Volume 4
of fifteen volumes

LIFE AROUND US

CHILDCRAFT

The How and Why Library

FIELD ENTERPRISES EDUCATIONAL CORPORATION

Chicago   London   Rome   Sydney   Toronto

Acknowledgments

The publishers of CHILDCRAFT—THE HOW AND
WHY LIBRARY gratefully acknowledge the following publisher for permission to use copyrighted
illustrations. Full illustration acknowledgments
for this volume appear on pages 362–363.

Time, Inc.: photography by Andreas Feininger, pages 104–
105, courtesy *Life* Magazine, copyright 1953 by Time,
Inc.

Time, Inc.: photography by John Dominis, page 163,
courtesy *Life* Magazine.

CONTENTS

VOLUME 4 *Life Around Us*

Living Things

You are living,
and wherever you go you'll find other living things.

Trees are living things,
and so are chattering squirrels that peek from the leaves
or crows that croak from the branches.

Grass is a living thing,
and so are ants and beetles that scurry through it
or lambs and foals that gambol on it.

Black-eyed Susans and forget-me-nots are living things,
and so are the honeybees and the butterflies
that flit and flutter around them.

Living things can be puppies whose feet seem too big,
or kittens chasing their own little tails.
Living things can be croaking frogs
and darting dragonflies, apple trees and daffodils,
wasps or worms, or tucked-in turtles—
even plants and animals too small to see.

How many living things can you find in this picture?

GIANT
PLANTS
AND
ANIMALS

Some plants and animals are big.
Some are bigger,
and some are so big, they make other living things look small.

A giraffe is so tall
it can nibble leaves even from high branches of a tree.

An elephant is so big
each leg is as thick as some tree trunks.

A giant redwood tree is so big
a tunnel for cars can be cut through it.

A whale is the biggest animal of all.
It is so big that it can be as long as three boxcars
and nearly as high as two elephants.

An ostrich is such a big bird that
you can put a saddle on it and ride it
in a race.

A giant turtle is too slow for a race,
but it's big enough for you to sit on and ride.

One animal is so big and roly-poly,
it would fill six bathtubs and still bulge over.
It's not only big but it has a big name, too.
It's the hippopotamus.

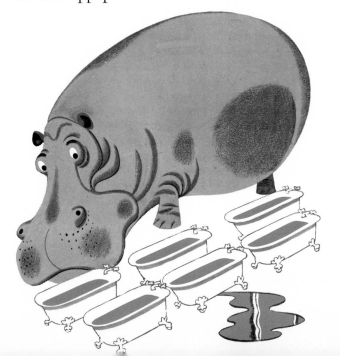

HOW SMALL CAN PLANTS AND ANIMALS BE?

Some plants and animals are small,
some are smaller,
and some are so small you can't see them at all.

You might call a honeybee small,
but a mite is much smaller.
It is so small it can hide in the fur of a honeybee.

You might call a mosquito small,
but a gnat is much smaller,
for it is as small as a speck of dust.

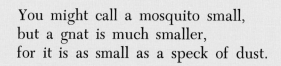

You might call a minnow small,
but a tiny goby found in the Philippines is much smaller,
for it is smaller than the head of a thumbtack.

You might call a violet small,
but an alga is smaller,
for it is small enough to grow inside a flea.

You might call a mouse small,
but a pygmy shrew is much smaller,
for it is so small it weighs less than a penny.

All these are small animals,
but they are not the smallest.
Can you see an amoeba or paramecium here?
No, they are so small you can't even see them.

HOW LONG DO PLANTS

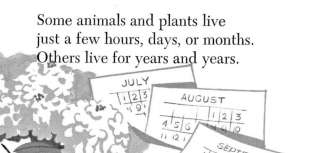

Some animals and plants live
just a few hours, days, or months.
Others live for years and years.

May flies live just a few short hours
or a day or two at most.
But houseflies and fruit flies
live for one or two months,
and candytuft plants live longer than that.

House mice may live to be three years old,
and bluejays till they're four.
But starfish and snails
can live till they're five,
and guinea pigs till they're six.

AND ANIMALS LIVE?

Elephants and ravens,
butternut trees,
and huge hippopotamuses
may live as long as people do.
But bulky box turtles
and giant sequoia trees
can live much longer than people.
Sequoia trees live for years,
       and years,
         and years,
           and years.

11

Coming into the World

All plants and animals have a mother.
But not all plants and animals are born in the same way.

Some animals like beavers, bats,
    and long-necked giraffes are born alive from their mother.

Other animals like barn owls, bumblebees,
    and Hawaiian butterfly fish are born from an egg.
    But it's a mother that lays the egg.

Some plants like oak trees, thistles,
    and bright yellow buttercups are born from a seed.
    But it's the mother plant that makes the seed.

Other plants like ferns, moss,
    and brightly colored mushrooms are born from a spore.
    But it's the mother plant that makes the spore.

Most baby plants and animals come
from grown-up plants and animals that are like them.

animal babies

Animal babies are all shapes and sizes—
Plain, striped, or spotted, and full of surprises!
But one thing, you see,
Which seems funny to me,
Is that most animal babies—gigantic or small—
Aren't really called babies at all.

A baby dog is called a pup.
A beaver is a pup until it grows up.
A baby seal, too, has pup for its name.
That seems rather odd,
    for they just aren't the same.

Cats have kittens, all covered with fur,
Kittens that mew, kittens that *purr-r-r-r*.
Bobcat babies are larger, it's true,
But all their babies are kitty cats, too.
But of all that are called kittens,
    there is one that is funny,
"Kitten" is the name of a soft, baby bunny.

A baby camel's a colt
    when it's new.
Some horses are colts
    when they are young, too.
Donkeys have colts.
    So do zebras with stripes.
Colts are all babies of similar types.

The graceful gazelle is a kid when it's new,
And the baby goat is a little kid, too.
Goats and antelopes
    are kids when they're small.
When they grow up—
    one is short, one is tall!

All ducks and all geese have little *lings*
Tacked onto their names
till they take to their wings.
Oh! Ducklings and goslings—and *swanlings*,
you'd bet?
No! Little swan babies
are always cygnets.
Now, birds have their *lings*,
but *birdling* is wrong.
They're *nestlings*, then *fledglings*,
until they are strong.

animal babies (continued)

Lions and tigers and bears may be wild,
But their babies, called cubs, are gentle and mild.
The high-yipping fox and the wolf with its howl
Also have cubs. So do sharks on the prowl.
And the far-swimming walrus, the nicest of all,
Has babies called cubs as long as they are small.

The babe of a cow is always called "calf,"
And so is the long-necked baby giraffe.
And calf is the name of a baby rhinoceros,
And also the name of a young hippopotamus.
The elephant baby's a calf that's not small,
But the calf of a whale is the largest of all.

JOYCE LAMENSDORF

How MANY babies will there be?

When animal mothers have babies, some have just one. But some have many. And some have more than you can count. Cows, camels, and gorillas (and some other kinds of animals) usually have only one baby at a time.

Rats, cats, dogs, bats, and bluebirds (and many other kinds of animals) have babies in bunches.

How BIG will the baby be?

You can't always tell how big an animal baby will be by looking at its mother.

Some big animals may have small babies,
and some may have big ones.
Some small animals may have big babies
and some may have small ones.

A baby blue whale is longer than a pickup truck,
but a polar bear baby will fit in a shoe.

A kitten can curl in the palm of your hand,
but a baby opossum will fit on your thumbnail.

A baby kiwi bird would cover a saucer,
but a chick could flap its wings in a teacup.

A horse has a baby that's as tall as a table,

Spiders and flies (and many more kinds of animals) have more babies than there are apples on an apple tree. And a salmon has more babies than there are leaves on a tree. A queen bee has one of the largest families of all because the queen bee never stops having babies. She has one after the other—one at almost every blink of your eye—for as long as she lives.

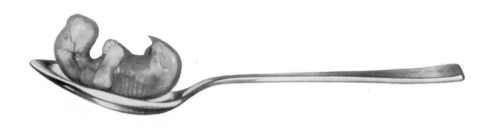

but a kangaroo baby could lie in a teaspoon.

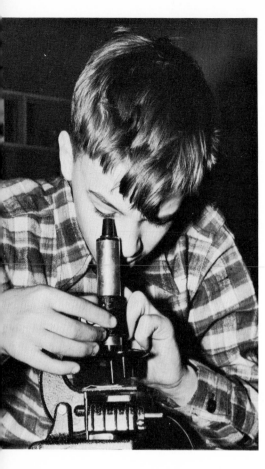

SOME
ANIMALS
SPLIT
IN TWO

When you grow,
you just grow and grow
until you get to be a grownup.
But some animals grow just so
much and then split in half
and become two animals.
Then the two animals keep
growing, just so much, until
they both split in half and
become four animals.
They never become big animals.
They just become more animals.

An amoeba is an animal that splits.
It is a tiny animal so small you can't see it.
It usually lives in pond water.
An amoeba eats
    and eats—
    and as it eats, it grows
            and grows.

But still it is so small that it never grows to be even
as big as a pinpoint!
When it has grown enough, it splits in two
and becomes two tinier amoebas,
which must eat
    and grow
    before they can split and become two again.

Some plants split in the same way
that animals like amoebas do.
They are called green algae.
They are also tiny and live in pond water.

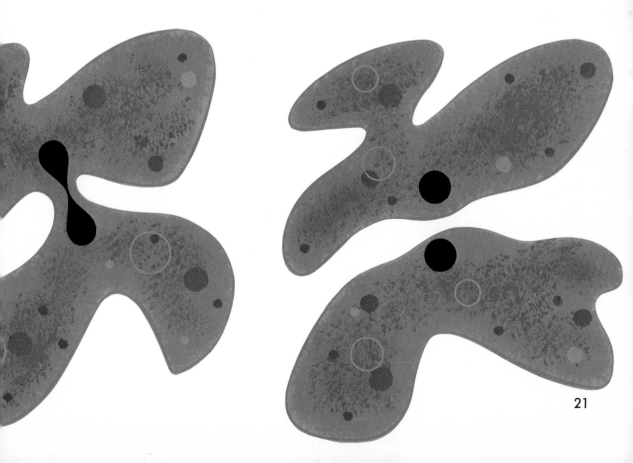

HATCHED FROM AN EGG

A baby chick is born from an egg
that comes from inside the mother.
When the egg leaves the mother's body,
we say that she "lays" it.
The hen sits on the egg and keeps it warm.
While she sits, the chick inside the egg grows,
and grows,
and grows,
and grows,

until it is so big that it fills the whole egg.

Now the chick is ready
to come out of the egg.

It pecks,
and pushes,
and pushes,

until it has pecked
and pushed
and broken the shell.

The chick has "hatched."

All baby birds
hatch from eggs
the same way
that the chicken hatches.

Crocodiles, turtles,
and most fish and snakes
hatch from eggs, too.
The difference between birds
and these animals
is that the mother
doesn't sit on the eggs
to keep them warm.
She lets the sun warm them.

WHERE DO PLANTS COME FROM?

Did you know that
hard, hairy coconuts are seeds?
So are wrinkled walnuts,
and orange pips,
and bright red strawberries,
and acorns!
A seed is a baby plant.

Inside an acorn
is a tiny tree trunk,
  a root,
  a bud,
  and two tiny leaves,
  so tiny you can hardly see them.
The baby oak tree is packed in a shell surrounded with food.
After an acorn falls on warm, damp ground, the shell gets soft.
Then the tiny trunk inside the shell gets longer and stronger,
and the soft shell breaks open.
The roots that were inside grow down into the ground,
and the baby bud and the baby leaves can now grow up
toward the light of the sun.
An oak tree has been born!

When is a seed not a seed?

If you saw some greenish-bluish stuff on an old piece of bread,
you would probably say, "That's moldy," and throw it away.
But did you know that mold is really a plant?
It is not a plant that grows from a seed,
but a plant that grows from tiny bits of powder called spores.

bread mold

Mushrooms with names like little helmet,
puffball, and jack-o'-lantern grow from spores, too.

little helmet

puffball

*common
mushroom*

The spores come from underneath the umbrella part
of a grown-up mushroom.
The spores may be blown off by the wind
or brushed off by a passing deer mouse
or another small animal.
But whether they are blown off
or brushed off,
each spore will grow into a
mushroom if it lands
on warm, damp earth.

jack-o'-lantern

BORN IN SACKS
AND BAGS

Baby spiders rock in a cradle that is a silken sack. A baby spider is born inside the sack with hundreds of other spiders. Like many babies, a baby spider is hungry as soon as it is born. It must eat or it will die, but there is nothing in the sack but other baby spiders.

Suddenly, something grabs the spider. It is one of the other spiders, and it is hungry, too. The two spiders fight. They fight silently— groping and grasping, writhing and twisting— until one of the baby spiders is dead. Now the winner has something to eat.

But to live and grow, the baby spider must fight again. The stronger babies keep eating the weaker babies until only a few spiders are left to crawl from the sack.

baby spiders in silken sack

Spiders are not the only animals born in sacks or bags.
A baby skate is a fish that is born in a mermaid's purse.
The bag with the egg inside it comes from the mother fish.
If you live by the sea, you may find a mermaid's purse
washed up on a beach.

mermaid's purse

28

A dogfish is born in a bag, too.
The dogfish bag hangs between seaweed stems.
It looks like a little hammock.
As soon as a dogfish hatches out of the bag,
it can take care of itself.

dogfish bag

Siamese fighting fish

Born in bubbles, nests, pockets, and mouths

Imagine being born in a nest made of bubbles of air!
Baby Siamese fighting fish are.
They are born from eggs that are in a nest
of tiny glistening bubbles that bob on top of the water.
The father fighting fish is the one that blows the bubbles.
Now and then some bubbles burst before the eggs can hatch.
Some of the eggs start to sink in the water!
But the father is watching.
He quickly catches the eggs, carries them back
to the surface, and blows them back into the nest.
When the eggs hatch, the bubbles burst,
and baby Siamese fighting fish come into the world.

A bubble nest may seem to be a strange place
for fish to be born.
But some fish are born in a mouth,
    some in a pocket,
    and some even in an underwater nest.
Egyptian mouthbreeders hatch from eggs in the mother's mouth,
but one kind of catfish hatches in its father's mouth.
A father sea horse has a pocket on its stomach for hatching eggs.
And sticklebacks' eggs hatch in a nest—
    an underwater seaweed nest.

sea horses

31

Born from eggs you can't see

The eggs you know most about are the ones you can see,
but many animals are born from eggs that you can't see
because these eggs are inside the mother.
Kittens, elephant calves,
and lion cubs are some of the animals
that are born from eggs inside their mothers.
People are, too.
Each of these babies grows inside its mother
until it is big enough to be born.

Almost all snakes hatch from eggs you can see.
But a baby rattlesnake
is born from an egg you can't see.
The baby rattlesnake leaves its mother's body
in a bag of skin so thin you can see through it.
The baby snake soon splits the sack and slithers out.

Almost all fish are born from eggs you can see.
But some fish are born from eggs you can't.
A mother rainbow fish, or guppy, carries eggs inside her
until they hatch.
Then the baby guppies leave her body
and wiggle out into the water.

HELPLESS BABIES

A baby boy and a baby girl are helpless when they are born.
So is a baby raccoon.
Baby raccoons are too weak even to raise their heads.
They cannot see,
but they huddle close to the warmth of their mother.
Then with warm licks and gentle prods from nose and paws,
their mother draws them nearer and feeds them her milk.
If you were close by and stood very still,
you might hear their cries—soft as a whisper—
coming from the hole at the top of the tree where they were born.
Whaaa—whaaa! They sound something like you did
when you were a baby!
It is many weeks before the young raccoons
are big enough and strong enough
to climb down from the hole in the top of the tree.

Many other animals are helpless when they are born.
Kittens, puppies, and baby rabbits, monkeys, and mice
all need their mother's help until they grow big enough
to take care of themselves.

BABIES THAT NEED
A LITTLE HELP

When you were a baby,
it was a long time before you could sit up—
and even longer before you could crawl or walk.
A baby deer—or fawn—can frolic,
run, and jump a few days after it is born.
But it still needs its mother's care.
A fawn is born deep in the woods.
At first it lies still, nestled in leaves,
while the mother washes it gently with her tongue.
Then slowly, with a blink of its big brown eyes,
the fawn raises its head
and struggles to stand on its four slender legs.
The fawn is hungry.
It stumbles to its mother,
and seeks her milk with gentle nudges.
Soon the fawn tires
and nestles back in the leaves to sleep.
After a few days, the baby deer is strong enough
to romp in the woods.

Baby cows, camels, and giraffes are other animals
that can romp and play soon after they are born,
but they still need their mother's help.

BABIES THAT

NEED NO HELP

Pudgy puppy dogs
and tiny cat kittens are helpless when they are born.
But baby turtles aren't helpless at all.
They know what to do as soon as they hatch.

Baby turtles know how to walk
and how to swim.
They know what to eat
and where to find what they eat.
They know they must find water
and where to go to find it.
They know when to shrink and hide in their shells
and when it is safe to come out again.
So the mother turtle doesn't have to nurse,
or teach, or protect her young turtles.
She just lays her eggs under sand and lumbers slowly away.
The sun warms the sand,
and the sand warms the eggs
long after the mother has gone.

Worms, grasshoppers,
and many kinds of fish also can take care of themselves
as soon as they are born.

Growing Up

As you grow up, you change in many ways.
It is the same with plants and animals.
An animal or a plant grows until it is
as proud as a peacock,
or as sweet as a nut,
or as strong as a bull,
or as swift as a deer,
or as big as an ox,
or as tall as a tree,
or as fat as a pig,
or as fierce as a lion,
or as graceful as a cat,
or as sly as a fox,
or until it is as grown-up as it can be.
On the next pages you will see
how plants and animals change as they grow.

GROWING UP IN A POUCH

Baby opossums are carried wherever they go.
First, they are carried in a pouch—
a fur-fuzzy pouch that looks like a pocket
on their mother's stomach.
The tiny opossums stay snug in the pouch,
feeding on their mother's milk
while she scurries around hunting for food,
    climbing trees, even swimming streams—
    just as though she had no family at all.

As the young feed, they grow.
Soon the young opossums are big enough to peek from the pouch,
    but still they don't climb out.
They keep feeding and growing
until they get big enough to run, climb, and swim.
Their mother still carries them
even when they are too big to be carried in the pouch.
So they ride piggyback—
clinging to their mother's fur with tiny claws.

Finally, they get too big to be carried any more—
even piggyback.
The time has come for them to leave their mother
and to take care of themselves.

close-up of baby opossum in mother's pouch

THE
OLDEST BABY

What is still a baby when foxes and wolves have lived their lives and cats and cows are getting old? And what is still a baby when an apple seed has grown into an apple tree and you've had more birthdays than there are fingers on your hands?

It is a cicada!

A cicada spends most of its life as a baby. A tiny cicada—or nymph—burrows into the ground as soon as it is born.

It stays in the ground—tunneling, creeping, and feeding for years and years and years—for seventeen years, in fact.

Finally, after winter has come and gone seventeen times, the nymph crawls from the ground, climbs onto a bush, splits its skin, and creeps out as a young cicada to *z-z-z-z-z-z-z-z-z-zip* from tree to tree.

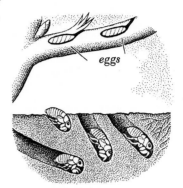

nymph going into ground

growing and tunneling

emerging from its skin

A
CHANGE
OF SKIN

Just as you get too big for your clothes as you grow, so, too, do animals get too big for their skins as they grow.

One animal that gets too big for its skin is a toad called a Bufo bufo. As the Bufo bufo eats, it grows and grows. And as the Bufo bufo grows, its skin gets tight—so tight that it can't get any tighter. So the skin starts to split down the toad's back.

The Bufo bufo starts rubbing off the old skin with its front feet. It rubs its neck, and it rubs its head—rubbing and rolling the old skin off its body. At last, squirming and struggling, the toad kicks its legs free. Then the Bufo bufo, shining in a bright new skin, swallows the old skin in one enormous gulp.

Toads are not the only animals that grow out of their skins. Lizards, salamanders, and snakes do, too. Snakes usually wiggle headfirst out of the old skin, but old skin on lizards just drops off in tiny pieces.

My! How a baby

It would be strange if a young mouse grew up to be an elephant, or a kitten grew up to be a kangaroo, or a young robin grew up to be a swordfish, or you grew up to be a turtledove.

But a baby caterpillar does something almost as strange. When it is a very small caterpillar, it eats and eats until it grows into a big caterpillar. Then, one day, the caterpillar starts to spin some silk. It spins and spins until it has spun a silk sack around itself. The silk sack is called a cocoon. The caterpillar stays in its cocoon until it gets so big that it cracks open the cocoon. Then something pushes, and struggles, and crawls out. Do you think the animal that crawls from the cocoon is a caterpillar? No! The caterpillar has become a beautiful moth!

can change

HOW DOES A TREE GROW?

A tree doesn't stretch when it grows.
It just adds new parts each year.
A tree gets taller
by growing new twigs at the ends of old twigs—
just as a pile of toy blocks gets higher
when you put one block on top of another.
Wrinkled lines mark the place
where a twig started growing each year.

A tree gets wider
by growing a layer of wood under the bark each year—
just as a line of blocks gets wider
when you put one beside another.
When a tree is cut down,
you can read its life story from the layers of wood that look
like rings spreading out from the middle of the trunk.
A tree grows dark rings in summer
and light rings in spring.
It grows a wide ring for showery and sunny years
and a narrow ring for dry and shady years.

FOOD FOR THE YOUNG

When you were a baby, you sucked your milk or you were fed with a spoon. But you never lapped or pecked your food, or had it pumped or stuffed into you. But some baby animals do.

Food That Is Stuffed or Pecked

Many bird parents stuff food down the throats of their young. But a young pelican pecks its food from a pouch under its parent's bill. The mother or father eats first. Then it squeezes what it eats back into its pouch. The young pelican puts its head into the pouch and pecks and pecks until all the food is gone.

Pump Fed

Young pouter pigeons are pumped full of pigeon "milk." The mother or father pumps the "milk" from its throat into the wide-open mouths of its young.

Lapping Food

Young platypuses lap milk from their mother's stomach. The milk oozes into furry dents that are shaped like saucers on her stomach. The young platypuses lap the milk from these dents, just as a cat laps milk from a saucer.

SWIMMING LESSONS

A puppy may never have to go into the water,
but it knows how to swim without being taught.
So it doesn't seem fair
that a baby river otter, which will spend most of its life
in the water, can't swim at all until it learns how.
A young river otter has to take swimming lessons
from its mother.

At first, the mother carries the young otter piggyback
as she rolls and twists,
and swims through the water.
Soon the young otter is used to the water.
Then, one day, the mother shakes the little otter off.
The young otter splutters and splashes.
It lashes its tail and paddles in the water
with four frantic paws.
The otter is swimming for the first time in its life!
But soon it is tired,
and the mother drags it back to the riverbank.
The swimming lessons go on for most of the summer,
until finally the young otter can swim
as well as its mother.
It can swim in a somersault chasing its tail
or float on its back while scratching its stomach.
Suddenly, it can dive—
swimming under water, leaving only a trail of bubbles
and a ring of widening ripples on top of the water.

PLAYING and ROMPING

A young seal plays in the largest swimming pool in the world— the sea. Young seals sometimes slide down a smooth sloping sand-bank and plunge headfirst into the sea with a sploosh. Down under the water they go—swimming and tumbling, and chasing each other in circles and somersaults.

Suddenly, with a swish of its strong flippers, one of the seals bursts out of the water into the air, then lands with a smack on its side. Another seal jumps. Then another and another until the water bubbles and foams. Young seals play in the sea for hours and hours. They splash and they snort. They bark and they blow bubbles as they romp and play in their huge swimming pool.

When you go to the zoo, look for the seals and see how much fun they have in the water.

ANIMAL GAMES

Animals play many of the games you play. Some play catch, some play hide-and-seek, and some even play leapfrog. Other animals dance and sing, and some just sit and make noises.

A kitten pounces on toys.
A puppy dog pounces
at its own shadow.
Baboons play by teasing
one another and by pulling
one another's tails.
And lambs chase butterflies
across a field.

Chimpanzees make swings from jungle vines. Otters build slides on a riverbank. Gorillas dance or pound their chests, and some kinds of monkeys and mice even sing.

A mockingbird plays at copying the songs of other birds. But a myna bird plays at copying you. It might say, *"Hello,"* or *"How-doyoudo,"* or *"I'mverywellthankyou."*

A family of martens sometimes play leapfrog with one another, and woodpecker families play hide-and-seek in a tree. Weasels chase each other, and a crane will toss and catch a stone with its beak.

Storks in Switzerland
build nests on special platforms
that people have above their homes.

LEARNING TO FLY

You might think that a bird can fly right after it is born.
After all, it is born with wings.
But a bird must learn to fly, just as you had to learn to walk.

A stork takes its first flying lesson
as soon as it is strong enough
to stand at the edge of its nest,
which is usually on a chimney top.
At first, the young stork stands still on its slender legs,
peering over the edge of the nest.
Then, ruffling its feathers
and flapping its wings,
the young bird struts slowly around the edge of the nest.
Suddenly, it starts hopping and flapping.
Around and around the nest it goes.

Hop-flap! Hop-flap! Hop-flap!

With each hop and flap,
the stork jumps a little higher
and hovers a little longer in the air.
The stork still cannot fly, but it is learning.
Then, with a powerful hop,
the young bird stretches its wings
and sails into the air.
It glides once around the chimney top
and lands back in the nest with a THUMP!
The stork now can use its wings. It can fly!

All birds that fly must learn to use their wings.
But they learn in different ways.
A mother falcon pushes her children from the nest.
A mother sparrow flies in front of her children with food.
The young birds reach for the food,
fall from the nest, and the next thing they know,
they are flying.

LEARNING TO HUNT

When many animals hunt, they are looking for other animals to eat. But more animals hunt for good plants to eat—like berries or nuts.

Bears even hunt for honey. When bears are young cubs, they must learn where to find honey. Here is one way they learn.

Two bear cubs are wrestling, clasped in a ball of brown fur. They roll, and tumble, and bump into a log, which gives off a scary buzz. The cubs sniff the

log and are frightened by the buzz. But before they can run away, their mother's big nose nudges them aside. Then her large paw rakes a hole in the log. She has heard the buzz, buzz, buzz of bees that make honey. And all bears—big bears and little bears—like honey

Bees burst out of the hole and swarm around the bears. But bee stings can't get through a bear's thick hair. So the bears take no notice of the bees except for an occasional swat. They dip their paws into the honeycomb and eat the honey—bees and all!

The bear cubs have had their first lesson in hunting honey. The mother also teaches them how to catch mice and how to slap fish and frogs out of the water.

CHASING OUT THE BABY

When you are grown up,
you can stay with your family until you are ready
to have a home of your own.
Even when you have your own family,
you will still be able to visit your parents.
But many young animals, when they have grown up,
are chased away by their parents
and never see them again.

Grown-up young lions might be chased away by a roar,
young bears by a growl,
and kangaroos by a cuff.
Young pigeons might be chased away by a peck,
young swans by a pinch,
foxes by a nip,
and a young moose by a kick from its mother.

Many animal parents chase their grown-up children away
before the next baby is born.

Finding
Things To Eat

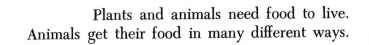

Plants and animals need food to live.
Animals get their food in many different ways.

Bears snatch.
Falcons grab.
Lions creep.
Giraffes reach.
Kingfishers dive.
Pintail ducks bob.
Spiders trap.
Turtles snap.
Walruses sift.
Robins pull.
Anacondas squeeze.
Anteaters lick.
Sunbirds suck.

Some animals eat only other animals.
And some eat only plants.
But some eat both plants and animals.

Some plants eat animals.
And some plants live on other plants.
But most plants make their own food.

67

Creeping
up
on
food

When members of the cat family go after food, they creep quietly toward their prey. It doesn't matter whether the cat is a big cat like a leopard, lynx, puma, jaguar, lion, or a big Siberian tiger, or a small cat like a bobcat. All these cats are hunters.

A tiger creeps up on a big antelope the way a house cat creeps up on a mouse. The tiger crouches low. It moves slowly and quietly until it is close to the antelope. Then the tiger runs and leaps, extends its claws, and pounces on the unsuspecting antelope.

The cat's padded paws, its keen hearing, and its sensitive whiskers, help it to be almost silent as it creeps around in search of food.

Animals that eat their food two times

You eat your food only once.
But a giraffe eats
the same food two times.
It bites leaves off trees
and swallows them whole.
The food goes down
its long neck
into its stomach
which has four parts.
In part of the stomach
the food is softened
into globs called cuds.

Later, while the giraffe
is resting,
the stomach muscles push
the cuds up
the giraffe's long neck
and back into its mouth.

Now the giraffe
chews the cud
and swallows it again.
The chewed cud goes back
down its long neck
and into another part
of its stomach.

Cows, sheep, goats, and deer
are other animals
that have four stomach parts
and that chew cuds.

71

THE ELEPHANT'S TRUNK

It hugs its baby.   It trumpets.   It picks grass.   It carries tree trunks.

The elephant uses its nose to pick up food. A nose is what the elephant's trunk really is. With its trunk, the elephant pulls leaves off high trees. Then it curls back its trunk to put the leaves into its mouth.

Most of the time the elephant uses its trunk to get food. But it does many other things with its trunk, too.

It spanks the baby.   *It squirts water.*   *It smells danger.*   *It swats a bug.*

ANIMALS THAT BUILD TRAPS

Some animals make traps to get their food.
A marbled spider spins a silken web to trap its food.
After the spider spins its web, it goes to a hiding place.
It waits until a fly gets caught in the sticky silken threads.
Then the spider darts out of its hiding place,
crawls over the web to the trapped fly, and eats it.

A spider does not get tangled in its own web
because it knows where to walk.
The web is made of two kinds of silken threads.
The silken threads on the outside
and the spokes of the web are dry.
The inside circles of silken threads are sticky,
so the spider cleverly crawls along the dry silken threads.

THE ANT LION

The ant lion digs a hole in the sand to trap its food.
It buries itself at the bottom of the hole.
Only its jaws stick out.
If an ant crawls to the edge of the hole,
it slips and slides down the slippery sand
and falls into the ant lion's jaws.

animals that SQUEEZE their food

Some snakes coil around other animals and squeeze them to death.
Then they swallow them.
A boa constrictor first grabs hold of a rat
with its strong, sharp teeth.
Then it coils the rest of its body
around the rat and squeezes it.
It squeezes and squeezes until the rat stops breathing.
A boa constrictor, like other snakes, swallows its food whole.
Its jaws spread far apart to swallow animals
bigger around than itself.
Its skin stretches,
and the food makes a big lump
as it moves through its long, slender body.

A python also coils its body around an animal and squeezes it.
The python is one of the biggest and longest snakes.
Some are thirty feet long.
A python can squeeze a pig to death and swallow it whole.

boa constrictor

python

Animals
that suck for food

Some animals suck food the way you sip through a straw.
The little hummingbird sucks nectar from flowers.
It flits from flower to flower
and hovers like a helicopter above each blossom.
It beats its wings so fast
you can hardly see them.
The hummingbird sticks its long pointed beak down into a flower.
Then it sucks the nectar with its even longer tongue
that is hollow like a straw.

The mosquito pierces your skin to suck blood through its beak.
While it sucks, it shoots a fluid that makes your skin itch.

The butterfly sucks nectar from flowers through a long tube
that it can curl up when it is not eating.

CATCHING FOOD
WITH A
STICKY TONGUE

Some animals whip, flip,
stick, or poke
a long sticky tongue to get food.

An anteater sticks out its long sticky tongue
and licks up ants and termites that crawl on the ground.
But many ants and termites stay in their nests.
So the anteater uses its sharp front claws to rip open the nests.
It licks up the ants and the termites it uncovers.
Then it pokes its long sticky tongue
down into the winding tunnels to find more ants to eat.

anteater

80

aardvark

An aardvark, too, licks up ants and termites
with its long sticky tongue.

Toads and frogs flip out their sticky tongues
to catch small insects.

A chameleon whips out its long tongue and catches small insects
with the sticky knob at the end of its tongue.

EATING LEFTOVERS

Some animals eat only leftovers—
the half-eaten food that other animals leave behind.
They do not kill their own food.

A lion that kills a zebra will eat until it is full.
But while the lion is eating,
a flock of bald-headed birds sit high in the treetops,
watching,
just watching and waiting.

These are the vultures.
When the lion has finished eating and walks away,
the vultures swoop down
and rip and tear and eat the leftover meat.

While the vultures eat,
a hyena might be hiding in the bushes waiting its turn.
When the vultures fly away, the hyena comes out
and eats any meat left by the vultures.

Vultures and hyenas are animal garbage collectors
that help to keep the ground clean.

Jackals, California condors, and marabou storks
are other animals that eat leftovers.

Catching

food in flight

Did you ever try to snatch a rock from the ground or field a hot grounder in baseball at the same time you were moving fast? It's hard to do, but some birds do it quite easily to catch the food they eat.

A hawk can swoop down on small animals and grab them without stopping or touching the ground. It has keen eyesight, strong wings, powerful feet, and long sharp claws.

During the day it soars through the air looking for a mouse, a rat, a shrew, or some other small animal to eat. When it sees one, it swoops down and grabs it. Then it soars high into the sky again. It sits in a tree where it rips and tears the food apart with its strong hooked beak before swallowing it.

Owls also catch their food by swooping down to grab it. But most owls hunt at night and not during the day.

The frigate bird steals food from other birds while it is flying. If it sees a gull with a fish in its beak, the frigate bird pecks and nips and swoops and dives at the gull until the gull drops the fish. The frigate bird flies so fast that it can catch the fish before it hits the water.

85

Birds that find food
in water

Did you ever reach into the water and try to grab a moving fish with your hand? It is not easy to do. But many water birds do it. They grab fish with their beaks.

DUCKS BOB FOR FOOD

A mallard floats on the water and bobs for its food the way you might bob for apples. When you bob for apples, your face gets wet and you have to bob many times to get the apple. But the mallard easily takes water bugs and other small animals into its beak.

KINGFISHERS DIVE FOR FOOD

A kingfisher sits on a branch above the water and watches for small fish. When it sees one, it dives into the water to catch the fish with its pointed beak. Then the kingfisher flies back to the tree, flips the fish into its mouth, and swallows it.

kingfisher

PELICANS GRAB FOOD IN A POUCH

A pelican has a big pouch under its beak. It swoops down on a fish and scoops it up into the pouch. The pelican does not store the fish in the pouch. It swallows it.

FLAMINGOS SIFT MUD FOR FOOD

Around the edge of a flamingo's beak are fine hairs that look like a comb. The flamingo dunks its head upside down into the water and mud. And it sifts small animals from the mud through the comb on its beak.

Storks, herons, egrets, bitterns, swans, and boobies are other birds that get their food in water.

flamingos

A FISH THAT SHOOTS AT ITS FOOD

It's hard to shoot a fly with a squirt gun. But an archerfish shoots down flies with a squirt of water.

The archerfish swims near the top of the water. It peers through the water, looking for flies and other insects that might be buzzing around or resting on branches just above the water.

When an archerfish sees a fly, it aims carefully before squirting a stream of water at the fly. The water knocks the fly down, and the archerfish catches it and swallows it. The archerfish can shoot a stream of water several feet into the air to hit insects.

A FISH THAT FISHES

You may think that people are the only ones
who go fishing with a pole.
But deep in the ocean lives a kind of fish
that goes fishing, too.
And it looks as if it is fishing with a pole!
The "pole" is really a long feeler that looks like a fishing rod.
On the end of the feeler are little threads that wave and wiggle.
This is the bait, wiggling the way worms wiggle on a hook.

The threads light up like fireflies,
so that other fish can see them
in the dark at the bottom of the ocean.
The wiggly, little threads look like food to the other fish.
But when another fish comes near,
the fish with the feeler opens its big mouth
and gobbles up the other fish.
People who go fishing with poles are called anglers.
What do you think this fish is called?
You are right. It is an angler fish.

When the LARGEST

The blue whale has a mouth so big that there is room enough in it to set up a card table and chairs. The blue whale is the largest animal in the world. It can be as long as three railroad cars and weigh as much as twenty-five elephants. The blue whale is bigger than any dinosaur ever was.

But big as the blue whale is, the food it eats has to be very small. A blue whale has no teeth, so it can't chew big pieces of food. And its throat is so small that nothing bigger than an orange can get through it.

eat the SMALLEST

So it eats the tiniest plants and animals there are. These tiny things are called plankton. Plankton are so small that thousands of them will fit in a water glass. They float near the surface of the ocean.

Long, stringy plates, which are hard like your fingernails, hang from the top of the blue whale's mouth. These long, stringy plates are called baleen. The blue whale swims with its mouth open most of the time. As it swims, water and plankton pour into its mouth. The baleen is used like a strainer. The blue whale pushes its big tongue against the baleen to catch the plankton that are in the water. Then it spits out the water and swallows the plankton.

Tug of War

A starfish pulls and tugs to open clamshells for its food. A clam has a tough, strong muscle that clamps its shell shut. Even a big, strong man cannot pull the shell apart with his hands. But a spiny starfish can.

To open the clamshell, the starfish wraps its arms around it. Under each arm are stubby little tube feet that work like suction cups. Its tube feet stick to the clamshell. Then the starfish starts to pull. It pulls one side of the shell one way and the other side of the shell the other way.

The clam can hold its muscle
tight for a long time.
But the starfish can
pull and pull and pull
for an even longer time.
When the clam cannot hold
its muscle tight any longer,
the shell opens slowly,
The starfish eats the clam.

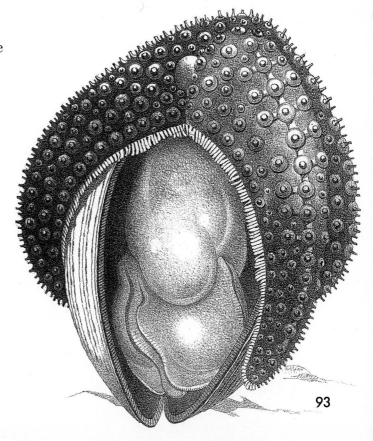

93

Animals
that wait for their food

Some water animals sit and wait for food to come to them.
Some stick themselves
  to lake bottoms,
    some to sea bottoms,
      some to ship bottoms,
        some to turtle shells,
          some to rocks,
            and others to whales.
              Then they wait.

fan worm

sponge

94

THE SPONGE

A sponge has many holes in its body so water goes through it easily. The sponge strains out tiny plants and animals from the water and eats them.

THE FAN WORM

A fan worm fans food and water into its mouth with feathery threads. It eats the food and shoves out the water. The rest of the worm's body is under the sand or mud at the bottom of the lake.

THE BARNACLE

A barnacle, which lives in a shell, waves its legs through the open shell to bring in water and food. It eats the food and pushes out the water.

THE SEA ANEMONE

A sea anemone waves stinging, barbed threads to catch its food.

THE ABALONE

An abalone whips and whirls long threads around to catch floating seaweed. Then it eats the seaweed.

barnacle

sea anemone

abalone

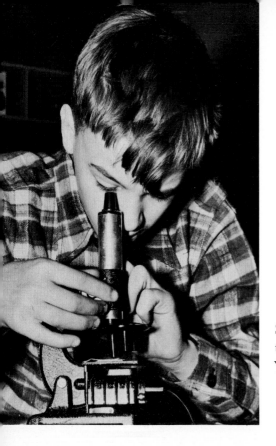

Getting
food
in a
water drop

Some animals are so tiny
that they can live in a single drop of water.
You cannot see them without a microscope.

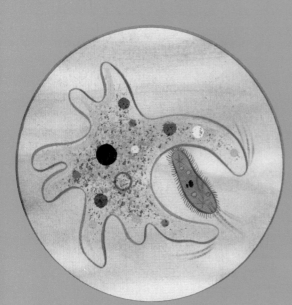

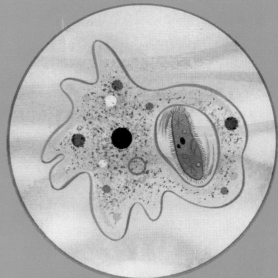

When a paramecium bumps into
an amoeba, it gets caught by the
jelly fingers of the amoeba.

The amoeba flows around the
paramecium. The paramecium
twists and jerks.

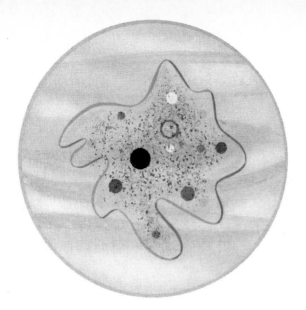

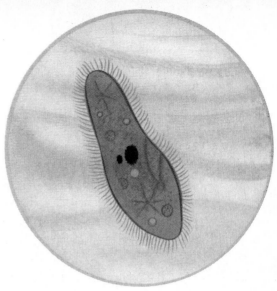

One of the tiny animals that can live in a waterdrop looks like a blob of colorless jelly. It is called an amoeba.

The amoeba eats other tiny animals that live with it in the drop of water. One of the animals it eats looks like a fuzzy bedroom slipper. It is called a paramecium.

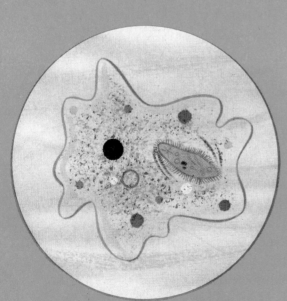

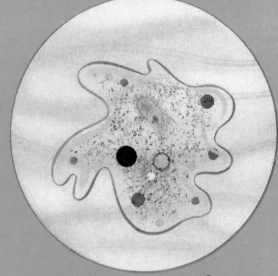

But the amoeba oozes down the sides and over the top of the twisting, jerking paramecium.

Finally, the creeping amoeba covers the paramecium completely. Now the paramecium is food for the amoeba.

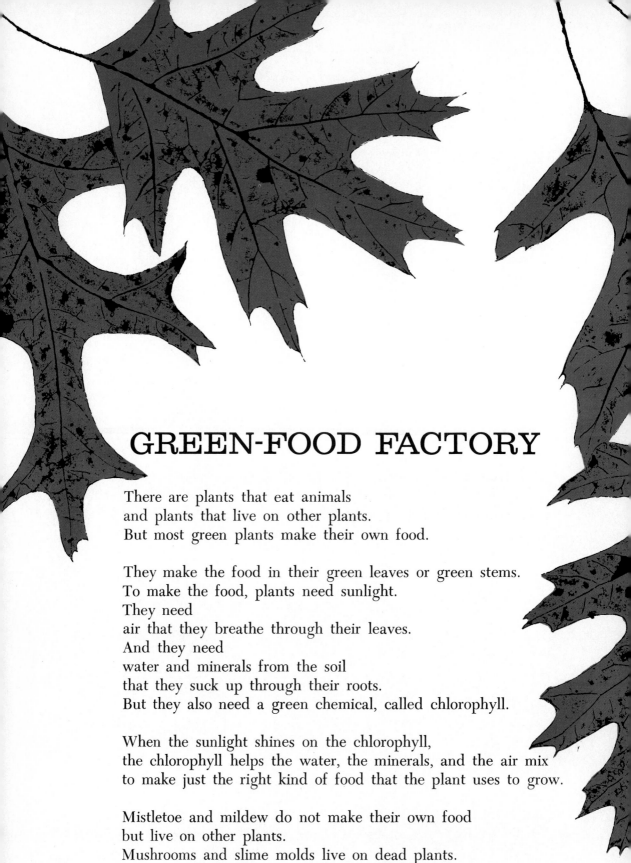

GREEN-FOOD FACTORY

There are plants that eat animals
and plants that live on other plants.
But most green plants make their own food.

They make the food in their green leaves or green stems.
To make the food, plants need sunlight.
They need
air that they breathe through their leaves.
And they need
water and minerals from the soil
that they suck up through their roots.
But they also need a green chemical, called chlorophyll.

When the sunlight shines on the chlorophyll,
the chlorophyll helps the water, the minerals, and the air mix
to make just the right kind of food that the plant uses to grow.

Mistletoe and mildew do not make their own food
but live on other plants.
Mushrooms and slime molds live on dead plants.

Magnified
cross section
of leaf

Some plants eat animals

These plants eat insects.
But how do they catch their food?
They can't walk.
They can't run.
They can't leap.

Here's how the
SUNDEW PLANT does it:

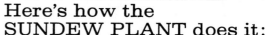

A fly comes buzzing by.
It sees some hairy leaves
sparkling with honey-like drops.
The fly circles and lights on a leaf.
But something is wrong.
The fly's legs are stuck
in the honey-like drops.
The drops are sticky and gooey.
They hold the fly tight.

The fly buzzes and jerks.
It flips and flops.
It pulls and twists.
But it can't get away.

The hairs on the leaf bend toward the fly.
And the sticky drops trap it.
The more the fly struggles,
the more it becomes tangled
in the hairs and the drops
until it smothers.

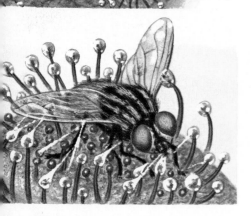

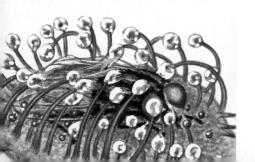

Here's how the VENUS'S-FLYTRAP does it:

On each leaf are six trigger hairs.
If a fly or other insect
touches the hairs,
the leaf snaps shut.
That is the end of the fly.

Here's how the PITCHER PLANT does it:

If an insect crawls too far
inside the pitcher plant leaf,
it cannot get out.
It falls into the rainwater
at the bottom of the leaf.
Then it drowns.

Where
Their Homes Are

Your home may be a house, or it may be an apartment.
Your home may be built of brick, wood, stone, or stucco.
But did you ever stop to think what makes it home?

Home is the place you always come back to.
Home is where your mother and father and maybe
your brothers or sisters are.
Home is where all members of the family eat, sleep, and play.
Home is your shelter from wind, rain, heat, and cold.
Plants and animals have homes, too.
Their homes may look different from yours,
but they are homes just the same.

Some are in holes in the ground.
Some are nests tucked in tree branches.
Some are like tunnels.
Some are like apartments with many rooms.
Some are holes in a hill, with secret passages.
Some are carried on the animal's back.
Some are right out in the open.
Some are made of mud, grass, or sticks.
But all are homes where animals and plants can grow,
stay, get shelter, and be with their families.

On the next pages you can visit many interesting
plant and animal homes.

Living in homes

A bat's home is a dark cave, or a barn, or an attic. It is so dark that the bat can't see where it is going when it darts around inside. Still, dark as a bat's home is, the bat can dart around in its home and never bump into the walls. How?

A bat finds its way by making high, shrill screeches as it moves. The sound of the screeches is so high that people can't hear the screeches. But a bat can hear its own screeches as they bounce and echo from the walls of its dark home.

If the sound of the screech bounces back quickly, the bat knows that a wall is near, and the bat turns away. The bouncing

without light

screeches that a bat makes work something like sonar or radar.

Some fish live in deep, dark caves, too. They have no eyes, for they have lived in darkness so long. But they can move around in the water without bumping into things. As they swim, they can feel the water around them quiver and shake. They know by the feel of the water waves when they are close to a big rock. The water pushes on them just a little more than usual, so they turn away. These fish are called blindfish.

Some other animals that have homes in dark places are worms, salamanders, white crayfish, cave rats, and cave crickets.

Homes under the ground

THE PRAIRIE DOG'S HOME

Imagine that you had to dive headfirst
   down a deep hole
    to get into your house!
That's what a prairie dog has to do.
When it gets to the bottom, it is in a tunnel.
The prairie dog sleeps and stores its food
in little rooms around the tunnel.
A prairie dog's home has only one opening.
It is above the ground at the top of a little mountain of earth.
This little mountain helps keep water
from running down into the hole.
The mound is also a good lookout post.
One of the prairie dogs in the family
sits on top of it and acts as a watchdog.

THE TRAP-DOOR SPIDER'S HOME

Even the richest kings and queens
didn't have all the walls of their castles
covered with silk.
But a trap-door spider does.
The home of a trap-door spider is a hole in the ground.
The spider crawls into it
and covers all the walls with its own spider silk.
Then at the opening the spider builds a door
out of mud mixed with some more of its silk.
When it goes in and out of its silky home,
it just opens and closes its trap door.
That's why it is called the trap-door spider.

Other animals that live in homes under the ground are
badgers, shrews, moles, foxes, and woodchucks.

Hideaway Homes

You probably have a secret hideaway that only you know how to find. But did you know that some animals have secret hideaways, too?

A coyote is an animal that has one. It makes its home on a mountainside. It is hard to find the opening because it is so well-hidden by bushes and rocks. The home is sometimes a little room at the end of a tunnel in the mountain. Sometimes the coyote makes a little hole in the ceiling of the room to let in fresh air.

An otter's secret is in its own home. The regular opening to an otter's home is a hole in a riverbank. But sometimes the otter also digs a secret door. The secret door leads to an underwater opening. If the otter has to get away from another animal, it can go in the regular door and out again through the secret door.

A bobcat hides its home behind many rocks, usually on a mountain ledge. Sometimes it makes its home in a cave.

109

Plants with watery homes

You may have seen a water lily floating on the water.
But did you know that you saw only part of the plant?
Most of it is underwater!

A water lily cannot make its home on dry land.
It needs lots of water.
It lives in lakes and rivers where its roots dig down into the
mud and sand on the bottom.

The leaves of the water lily float on top of the water.
They float so well that frogs
sometimes sit on them and don't sink.
The leaves of one kind of giant water lily, called Victoria regia,
are so large and strong
that even you could stand on them and not sink.

Seaweed is a water plant, too. It grows in lakes and oceans.
Sometimes you can see seaweed floating on top of the water.
But most of the time it grows only underwater
where you can't see it.
Some seaweed is green, some is red, and some is brown.

Other plants that make their homes in water are
the water hyacinth, the lotus, and the duckweed.

NESTS ARE MADE OF SCRAPS

Birds build their nests out of grass,
   or twigs,
     or string,
       or spider webs,
        or mud,
          or any other scraps that they can find.

The tiny hummingbird's nest
is fastened to a tree
with spider webs.
It is only as big as a silver dollar.

Orioles build hanging pouch nests
of string, grass, and bark.

Grebes build nests on top of water.

A meadow lark builds its grass nest
on the ground.
Sometimes it builds a grassy tunnel
leading to its nest.

Baltimore oriole nest

grebe nest

meadow lark nest

chimney swift nest

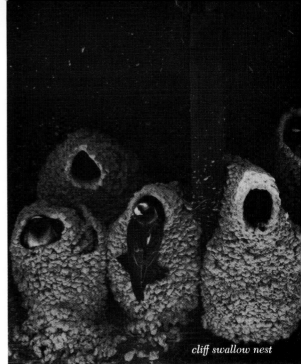
cliff swallow nest

The chimney swift builds
its nest of twigs in a chimney.
The nest looks like a little hammock.

A cliff swallow uses mud to build
a nest that looks like a bottle
tipped on its side.

The bald eagle builds its nest
of sticks and trash.

bald eagle nest

You may think that birds are
the only animals that live in nests.
But other animals build nests, too.
Squirrels, rabbits, deer mice,
field mice, and pack rats
aren't birds, but they build nests.

Sometimes a field mouse builds a nest
in the grass or in a big grain field.
Sometimes pack rats build nests
on rocky ledges or in clumps of cactus.
Pack rats pick up shiny buttons,
buckles, and rocks and hide them
in their nests.

113

Always water
in the basement

A beaver's home, called a lodge, always has a flooded basement. Beavers build their lodges on or near ponds or streams with one room above the water and one room off to the side and underwater. The only way a beaver can get into its lodge is to dive under the water and find the opening in the bottom room—the flooded basement.

An underwater tunnel leads from the flooded basement room to the top room where the beavers sleep and keep warm in the winter.

The beavers store sticks and twigs—their food for the winter—in the flooded basement. They push the food into the mud on the bottom of the pond, or they weigh the sticks down with rocks to keep them from floating away. When the pond is covered with ice and snow and the beavers cannot get outside, they still have enough food in the flooded basement.

When the water in the pond or stream is not deep enough to fill the basement, the beavers build a dam. The dam makes the water deep enough to cover the openings in the bottom of their lodge. And the water keeps dangerous land animals from getting into the beavers' home.

Muskrats build lodges that are very much like beaver lodges.

Trees have homes, too!

Where is a tree's home?
A tree's home is where it grows.
It is always a home with no roof—except the sky.
It is always a home with no walls—except the air.
It is always a home with just grass and dirt for a floor.

But different kinds of trees have their airy,
open homes in different kinds of places.

Your back yard may be the home of
an oak tree or a maple tree,
an elm tree or a poplar tree,
a sycamore tree or a birch tree,
or even a weeping willow tree.

But some trees can grow only where it is very dry.
The crooked Joshua tree grows in the desert.
And so does the saguaro cactus, which looks like a scarecrow.
And so does the mesquite,
the desert bramble bush that looks like a tree.

And some trees can grow only where it is wet.
A cypress tree looks as if it is sitting down
in a swamp with its knees in the air.
And mangrove trees grow at the edge
of salty oceans with their roots
sticking out of the water.

Pine trees grow on high mountains.
But if the mountain is very high,
the trees don't grow all the way to the top.
The place where trees stop growing is called the timber line.
The land above the timber line
is too cold for trees to grow there.

Date palms, fig trees,
coconut palms, betel palms,
eucalyptus trees, and rubber trees
all grow in low, hot places.

sloth

Animals that live in tree houses

It is fun to have a tree house, but you wouldn't want to live in a tree all the time the way some animals do.

One animal that makes its home in a treetop is called a sloth. It is an upside-down animal that lives in South America. The sloth hangs from tree branches, and it does everything upside down. The sloth is a slow-moving animal that almost never comes down from its tree house.

Most monkeys and apes make their homes in trees, too. Gorillas even build nests in the trees they sleep in at night. They break off branches and make springy mattresses out of them.

A koala makes its home in a special kind of tree—the eucalyptus tree. It holds onto the tree branches with its sharp claws.

koala bear

SAND-CASTLE

Ants live in sand castles that have many secret passages.
The passages lead to
   the nursery room,
     the storage room,
      the barn,
       the trash room,
        and many other rooms.

When the ants build the rooms and passages,
they take the grains of sand outside
and pile them into a big hill over the castle.

AND PAPER HOMES

Most wasps make their own paper.
And they build their nests out of it.
They chew wood and plants into furry globs
and build a nest out of the globs.
After the nest of globs dries,
it is something like the kind of paper you write on.
Hornets and yellow jackets make paper nests, too.
Other wasps make their nests of mud.
The potter wasp makes a nest of mud
that looks like a jug.

The mud-dauber wasp makes a nest of mud
    that looks like a bunch of pipes
        lying side by side.

Homes
on
their
backs

People who live in trailers take their homes with them. But did you know that some animals take their homes with them, too?

The snail's home is its shell. But the snail can never walk all the way out of its home because its body is attached to the shell.

A snail builds a door on its home by blowing a gooey bubble over the shell opening from the inside. When the snail wants to come out, it just breaks open the door.

Some other animals that carry their homes with them are turtles, clams, and oysters.

fresh—water clams

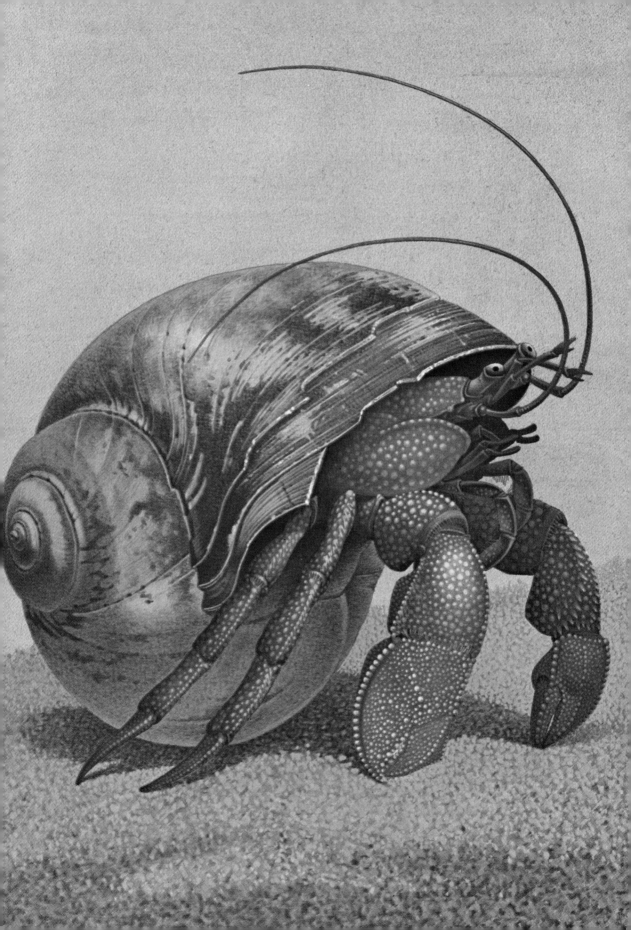

HOUSE ROBBERS

Some animals steal the homes of other animals
rather than build their own.

The hermit crab is such a house robber.
It steals snail shells—the homes that snails live in.
Even if a snail is in the shell,
a hermit crab will steal the shell.
It just pulls the snail out and eats it.
Then the crab twists its own body into the empty shell
so that only its claws stick out,
opening and closing like a door.
Inside the shell, the hermit crab grows.
When it grows to be too big for the snail shell,
the crab crawls out to look for a bigger shell to steal.

Other animals that steal homes are birds called burrowing owls
and four-legged animals called wart hogs and shrews.
The homes they steal are holes in the ground
that first belonged to foxes, aardvarks, or mice.

HOMES IN WORN-OUT TREES

What good is an old, dead tree? Look closely . . .

You may see
    a little masked raccoon sticking its head
      out of one of the holes in the tree.
You may see
    a frisky little squirrel storing nuts in it.
You may see
    a prickly porcupine peeking out of it.
You may see
    the wide-open eyes of an owl on one of its dead branches.
You may see
    a woodchuck or a skunk crawling out of it.
You may see
    a sleepy bear taking its long winter nap inside its trunk.
You may see
    a woodpecker peck, peck, pecking a hole in the side of its trunk.

Old hollow trees may be of no use to you.
But all these animals may make their homes in them.

A new home every day

Some animals live in a new home every day.
These are the many kinds of animals that live by
wandering around from place to place.
The place where they stop each day is their home for that day.
Some of their homes are out in the open,
   some are in bushes,
     some are under trees,
       some are even under the ground.

Zebras, antelopes, gazelles, and elephants
move from place to place in groups.
They usually move at night,
and sleep or graze out in the open during the day.

A tiger has a new home every day.
It wanders alone at night and sleeps in bushes during the day.

An earthworm has a different tunnel for a home each day.
It digs many tunnels through many miles of dirt.
When it stops in one place, that is home.
But it never stops for long.

Some other animals that have a new home every day are
walruses, fish, whales, and rhinoceroses,
buffaloes, deer, giraffes, and hippopotamuses.

Moving Around

Fish swim,
birds fly,
frogs jump,
and dogs walk.
But some plants and animals
move in stranger ways.
Turtles creep on the ground.
Monkeys swing through the trees.
Water bugs skim across the water.
Plant seeds sail through the air.
Moles tunnel under the ground.
Rabbits hop.
Snails slide.
Jellyfish float.
Tumbleweed rolls and tumbles.
Flying squirrels glide from tree to tree.
And some plants and animals go places
only when they are carried
by other plants and animals.

WHO MADE THESE TRACKS?

You don't have to see a rabbit hopping,
or a horse galloping,
to know that animals move around in different ways.
You can see animal footprints left in the snow,
in soft mud,
or in loose sand.

When you see these footprints,
you know a dog walked here.

Or if you see these funny tracks,
a bird was here.

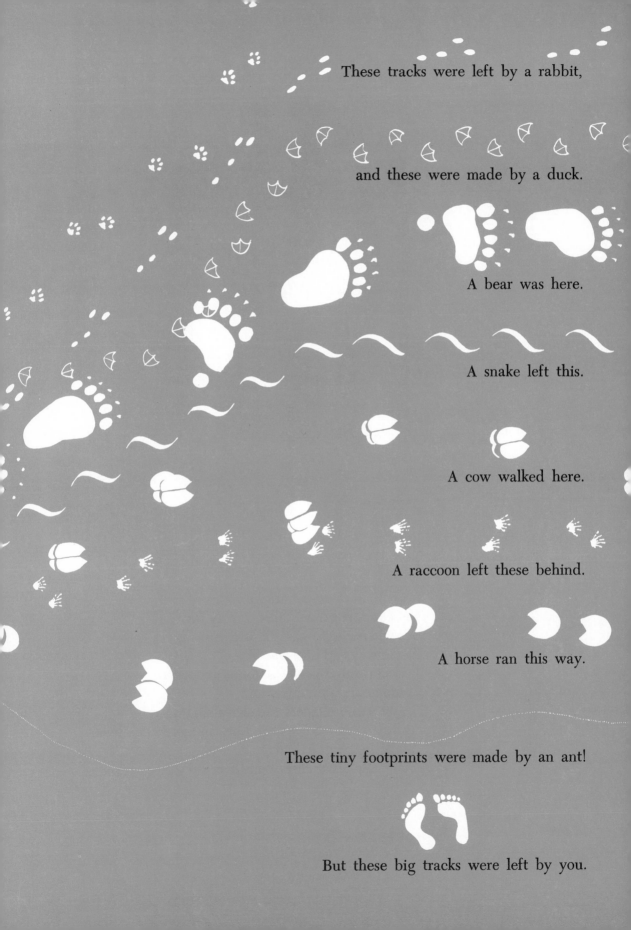

These tracks were left by a rabbit,

and these were made by a duck.

A bear was here.

A snake left this.

A cow walked here.

A raccoon left these behind.

A horse ran this way.

These tiny footprints were made by an ant!

But these big tracks were left by you.

MOVING BACKWARD

BACKWARD SWIMMERS

If you had to walk backward,
you couldn't go very fast or very far.
But when crayfish and lobsters swim,
they always go backward.
They zip through the water at great speed,
leaving only a muddy trail.
Crayfish and lobsters can swim backward
because they have special tails that open like fans.
When these animals swim,
they make quick flips with their tails.

AND FORWARD

THE HELICOPTER BIRD

No other bird can fly in so many ways
as the hummingbird.
The tiny hummingbird can fly up,
  down,
    backward,
      forward,
        or it can just hover in the air—
          like a helicopter.
            The hummingbird can do
            all these things because its
            wings move in circles so
            fast you can't see the
            wings, just as you can't see
            the blades of a helicopter
            when it is moving.

THE CRAB MOVES SIDEWAYS

Here is an animal that couldn't walk a straight line forward
if it tried—so it always moves sideways!
The crab runs across the sand on the tips of its toes.
It can move almost as fast as you can walk,
even though it must go sideways.

Creeping along

SLOW AS A TURTLE

Land turtles are bowlegged. They walk with their toes turned in and their knees turned out. A turtle's legs are short and its body is heavy, so it can't move very fast. The turtle usually creeps along at a speed that seems slow to you, even if it is in a hurry! It is so much work for a turtle to move that it hardly ever goes far from the place where it was born.

A MEASURING WORM

The measuring worm curves its whole body in a loop every time it takes a step. To creep along a tree limb, the worm brings its back feet up to touch its front feet, making the loop. Then it lifts its front feet and stretches its body forward.

It takes so long for the measuring worm to take just one step that it moves only a short distance in a day. It is called a measuring worm because it seems to be measuring the distance it moves with each step.

PLANTS THAT CREEP

Even some plants move by seeming to creep.
The strawberry plant sends out runners, or vines,
that get longer and longer
as they creep along the ground.
When the growing season is over,
the ends of the strawberry vines are far from the mother plant.

A banyan tree seems to creep, too.
But it takes many years for it to move.
The banyan tree moves by growing new roots,
which hang down from its branches
and go into the ground below.
A single banyan tree may grow so many roots
that in time it covers a whole forest.

With a hop or a jump

JUMPING WITH LEGS AND TAIL

How high can you jump?—
not as high as a kangaroo!
A kangaroo can jump higher than it is tall
or leap forward three times its length
because it has such powerful legs and feet.
The broad tail of the kangaroo helps it to balance
when it jumps.
If a kangaroo's tail is hurt,
it can't jump well at all.

A HIGH JUMPER

A grasshopper can jump ten times
as high as its body is long.
And it can jump twenty times its length
across the grass.
If you could jump as well,
you could jump over your house.
The grasshopper has wings for flying, too,
but it usually jumps to move.

BEST JUMPER OF ALL

The flea is the best jumper of all animals.
A flea is so small you can hardly see it,
but it can jump the length of your arm in one hop.
If you could jump as well as a flea,
you could jump over a tall office building,
or across a wide river.

ROLLING AND TUMBLING

THE TUMBLING TUMBLEWEED

Tumbleweed only tumbles in the autumn. When strong winds blow across the plains, tumbleweed withers and breaks off from its stem near the ground. Then the wind tosses and tumbles the dried-up plant—sometimes for miles. Tumbleweed stops rolling only when it piles up against a fence or falls into a gully. But the tumbleweed has spread its seed as it scraped along the ground. Next year more tumbleweed will grow and break from its stem to be tumbled by the wind again.

MOVING BY SOMERSAULT

Can you turn a somersault in water? The tiny water animal called a hydra somersaults all the time. That's the only way it moves. The hydra is no longer than your thumbnail and no wider than a thread. It has no head, legs, or arms. But long threads grow out from one end. These threads help the hydra turn over and over as it somersaults through the water. When the hydra finds a rock or a plant to cling to, it stretches out its threads to catch its food.

A mole may be underground when you see tiny cracks in the earth.

PAUL McNEAR

Moving Underground

AN ANIMAL TUNNEL DIGGER

Did you ever try to dig a tunnel in your back yard?
Digging is hard work—even with a big steam shovel.
But a mole, which lives underground,
digs tunnels most of the time
looking for worms and insects to eat.
A mole doesn't need a shovel to help it dig.
It uses its pointed nose
and sharp claws to plow through the soil.
It uses its wide front feet
to scoop the loose dirt behind it and above it.
When the mole finds a worm,
it quickly gobbles it up,
and then it keeps digging until it finds another worm.
In one night a mole can dig a tunnel
longer than a garden hose.
Moles don't often come above ground.
Owls and foxes can catch moles easily
when they come out of their tunnels.

USING TUNNELS MADE BY OTHERS

The shrew is still another underground animal,
but it doesn't dig its own tunnel.
It moves through tunnels that have been dug by mice.
A shrew looks something like a mole,
but the smallest ones are so tiny
they weigh no more than a penny.

DIGGING BY EATING

An earthworm has no feet, no claws, no teeth, and no nose.
But still it digs tunnels.
The only way it can get rid of the dirt it digs is to eat it.
And that's just what it does!

Sliding and Slithering

A SNAIL BUILDS ITS OWN ROAD

A snail slides forward on a slick roadway
that has oozed from beneath its foot.
You may have seen the silver trail it leaves.
This roadway also protects the snail's soft body
as it travels over rough bark, stones, or twigs.
The silver trail built by the snail protects it so well
that it can even slide over the edge of a razor blade
without getting cut.

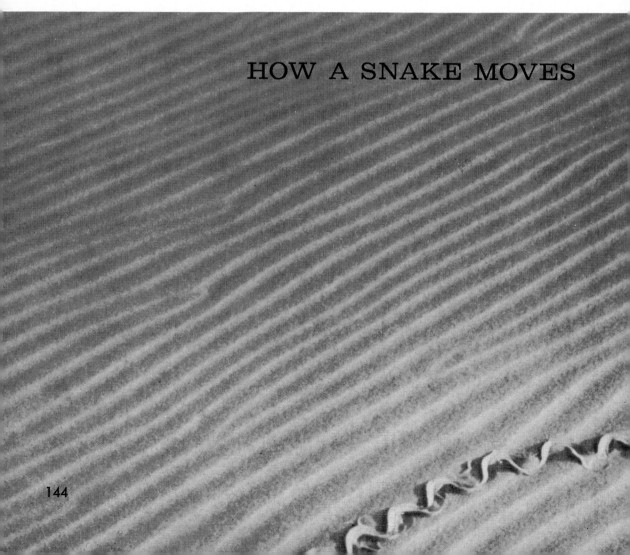

HOW A SNAKE MOVES

A snake can twist and bend its long body
into a circle,
or an "S" curve, or a coil,
or almost any shape.
A snake can bend and twist so well
because it has many joints along its body.
To move over the ground,
a snake bends its body into curves.
By pushing each curve against the hard ground,
or a rock, or a twig,
the snake can move fast.
Because the snake moves many parts at once,
it looks something like a streak of lightning.

SAILING AND FLOATING

SEEDS THAT SAIL AND FLOAT

Some plants and animals can't move by themselves,
yet they travel great distances through air or on water.

Some seeds seem to be made to sail or float.
Fluffy milkweed and dandelion seeds can sail through the air
like tiny parachutes.
Thin wings sticking out of maple and elm seeds
help them to glide through the air.
When these seeds fall into water,
the thin wings hold them up like water wings.
But whether a seed is blown away or floats away,
it usually ends up far from the mother plant.

PLANTS THAT FLOAT

The green patches you sometimes see on ponds and lakes
may really be masses of tiny plants.
They may be algae
or they may be duckweed.
They have long roots that hang down in the water.
Since the roots are not fastened to anything,
the plants are free to move with the waves.

AN ANIMAL THAT FLOATS

A jellyfish is a sea animal
that spends much of its life
floating on water.
It floats with the currents,
its long threads trailing
through the water to catch food.
But a jellyfish must go
where the water takes it,
and sometimes a jellyfish
is washed upon the sand.
There it will just dry up and die
because it can't move
to get back into the water.

FLYING WITHOUT WINGS

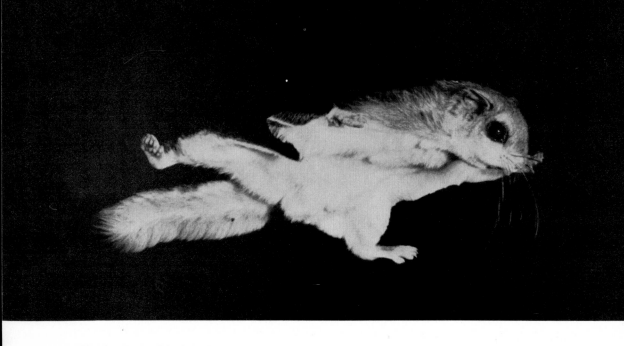

A SQUIRREL THAT FLIES

Squirrels don't have wings,
but one kind of squirrel seems to fly.
A flying squirrel has folds of skin that it uses as wings.
The folds are between its front and back feet.
The flying squirrel doesn't fly the way a bird flies.
It just glides.
When a flying squirrel jumps from a limb,
it stretches out its legs to open the folds of skin—
in much the same way you would open an umbrella.
The squirrel first glides down, down, down to get up speed.
Then it straightens out
and glides up, up, up until it reaches another limb.
When the squirrel wants to slow down or turn,
it uses its tail like the rudder of an airplane,
moving it to one side or the other.

FLYING FISH

The fins of all fish help them to swim,
but the fins of one kind of fish also help it to fly.
A flying fish flips itself out of the water
with its strong tail.
Then it spreads out the large fins at its sides
and glides through the air.
It uses its tail fins as a rudder to turn its body in flight.
Sometimes a flying fish will even glide the length of a big ship
before it slips back into the water.

They
swing
through
the air

THE JUNGLE ACROBAT

A spider monkey is the acrobat of the jungle.
It swings by its hands, hangs by its tail,
turns somersaults on the tree branches,
and does flips in the air.
It can swing from tree to tree
nearly as fast as a bird can fly.

This monkey can move fast
because it has a special tail that it uses as an extra hand
and because it has long, thin legs.
The spider monkey spends its life in the treetops.
It has no need to come down to the ground.

When it wants water,
the spider monkey hangs by its tail over a pond
and scoops up water in its cupped hands.

If it wants food, it lowers its long tail
into a bird's nest and pulls up an egg,
or it picks fruit and leaves from the trees.

SWINGING FROM A THREAD

When a spider moves to find a new home,
it first climbs up a fence or a tall weed.
Then it sends out a streamer of silk thread.
As the spider sends out a longer and longer thread,
the wind lifts the thread higher and higher in the air.
Soon there is enough thread to hold the weight of the spider.

The wind carries the thread away
with the spider dangling on the end of it.

When the spider wants to come down again,
it pulls in the thread.
As the thread gets shorter,
the spider slowly comes down to the ground.

water strider

SKIMMING AND SWIMMING

SKATING ON WATER

Did you know there are some animals that can walk on water?
One of these is an insect called the water strider.
This insect can walk on top of water without sinking.
It skims across the water the way a person skates on ice.
The funny thing is that a water strider can't swim.
The water strider would drown if a big wave washed over it.

duck

octopus

HOW THEY SWIM

Most animals that live in or near the water can swim.
But each animal has its own way of swimming.
A fish swims by moving its fins and tail.
A dolphin swims by flipping its tail.
An octopus darts around by drawing water into its body
and then shooting the water out behind it like a jet.
A turtle swims by moving all four legs.
A frog swims by kicking both hind legs.
A duck swims by paddling with its webbed feet.

Hitchhikers

ANIMALS THAT EAT WHILE THEY RIDE

Plants and animals don't ride on trains or buses the way you do, but some still take rides—on other animals.

Perhaps you've seen a dog scratching itself after it has brushed against weeds or after it has waded through water. The dog scratches because a tiny animal, called a parasite, has hitched a ride on it.

A parasite is an animal that lives on other animals and gets its food by sucking the blood of other animals. It may be a louse or a flea that crawls over the dog's skin and bites when it is hungry. Or it may be a leech or a tick that bites only once—when it hooks its teeth into the dog's skin.

Parasites can have hitchhikers, too. Fleas can have smaller fleas, and lice can have mites that ride on them and suck their blood, too.

PLANTS THAT CLING WHILE THEY RIDE

The seeds of many plants travel to a new home by hitchhiking. Cockleburs, sticktights, and Spanish needles are seeds covered with barbs and hooks. They catch in the fur of passing animals.

Mistletoe seeds are sticky and cling to the beaks of birds. When these clinging seeds are rubbed off the animals, they drop far from the mother plant where there may be more room to grow.

When To Change Homes

Did you ever move from one house to another,
from one town to another,
from one country to another?
Sometimes animals leave their old home
and begin a long trip to a new one.
They may move together in herds and flocks
or travel alone.
They may go many miles
or only a short distance.
When animals change homes,
they move to a warmer place,
or they go to a place where there is more food,
or they go to a special place to have their babies.
And sometimes animals just move—
but we don't know exactly why.

The next pages tell about some animals that change homes.

IS THE LEADER
THE STRONGEST?

Wild geese sometimes fly in the shape of the letter "V" when they go south for the winter. The strongest goose in the flock may be the one that flies in front—at the point of the "V." This front goose cuts through the air and makes it easier for the others to fly. But when the front goose gets tired, it falls back into the "V." Then the next strongest goose takes the lead. The geese may keep changing places in this way throughout their journey to their winter homes.

Some other birds that fly south for the winter are robins, cranes, bluejays, thrushes, and kingfishers.

But not all birds fly south for the winter. Birds that live near the South Pole may fly north. And some may stay where they are.

Which way do the penguins go?

Some penguins go north
and some penguins go south
when they move to their winter homes.

Emperor penguins walk toward the South Pole.
But smaller penguins, called Adélie penguins,
walk to the sea—away from the Pole.
They walk over ice and snow,
through blizzards and high winds,
and even slide down snowdrifts on their stomachs.

When they find the nests they used the year before,
the emperor penguins stop to lay their eggs
and raise their young—
usually during the coldest part of the winter.
But Adélie penguins do not lay their eggs until spring.
They spend their winters swimming in the icy sea.

161

THEY EAT
WHILE
THEY SWIM

How would you like to eat
all your meals while swimming?
That's what fur seals do!
They live way out in the middle
of the ocean most of the year.
The only times they come to land
are when they are sick or hurt.
But when the ocean warms up in the spring,
they swim thousands of miles
to rocky beaches to have baby seals.
When the baby seals are big enough to travel,
the seal families go back
to the middle of the ocean
where they romp and play all winter.

HALFWAY AROUND THE WORLD

Whales live in the ocean all the time, too.
One kind of whale, the whalebone whale,
swims halfway around the world every year
to find enough food to eat.

They don't like deep snow

Reindeer have to use their hoofs
to push away the snow
to find moss and other plants to eat in the wintertime.
When the snow gets to be as high as the reindeer's knees,
there's too much snow to kick away,
so they move to new feeding grounds.

Day after day,
they climb snow-covered slopes,
slide down deep ravines,
and swim through icy streams
as they search for patches of food.

As the reindeer travel, they stay close together,
jostling and pushing each other.
If each reindeer doesn't keep its head up,
its antlers will tangle with the antlers of another reindeer.
After a long journey they find enough food to eat until
summer comes.
Then the reindeer herds go back to their summer homes
because the snow has melted away.

Other animals that make long journeys overland
to new feeding grounds
are bison, caribou, and elk.

EVERETT McNEAR

SALT-WATER SALMON
FRESH-WATER BABIES

Salmon live their whole lives in salt water—except when they are born and when they die.

As soon as the time comes for them to have their babies, they look for a fresh-water stream. That means they have to swim a long, long way. And they have to swim against the fast currents of the rivers that rush into the sea.

Every year thousands of salmon start this long journey. They face many dangers. During the trip, some salmon are swallowed by larger fish, others are snatched up by sea birds, and some are caught in the nets and on the hooks of fishermen.

When they find a stream, the salmon swim upstream against the swift current. They even jump to the tops of waterfalls! Also, they must keep away from hungry bears because bears are good at catching salmon.

Finally, when they come to the end of their trip, they lay their eggs. Now they are all tired out from the long swim. They just give up and float tailfirst downstream. In a few days they die. But the new baby salmon go out to the salt-water sea again and live their lives—until it's time for them to have babies.

Eels swim together

Have you ever watched a crowd of people going into or coming out of a building? They stay close together as they move.

Baby eels also stay close to each other when they swim upstream to find a new home. When there are thousands of eels traveling together, they look like a long rope in the water.

An eel is a fish that is long and thin like a snake. Eels are born and die in the ocean, but many kinds spend most of their lives in rivers.

Though each baby eel is only about three inches long, baby eels can make a line more than a mile long when they swim together. As the eels swim upstream, they must go against a swift current. The farther they travel upstream, the shorter the line of eels becomes.

Some of the eels leave the others and go into ponds and streams along the way. Some get eaten by animals during the journey. The eels that reach their new homes stay there for several years.

When they are ready to have babies, they start swimming down the river to the sea again. When they reach the sea, they lay their eggs and die.

salt-water eels

fresh-water eels

BUTTERFLY TREES

Did you ever see a tree that looked as if
it had butterflies for leaves?
When monarch butterflies go south,
where the winters are warm,
they travel many miles during the day.
At night thousands swoop down on the trees.
Then the trees look as if they had butterflies for leaves.

The butterflies hang by their little hooked feet
upside down on the twigs.
They fold their wings tightly together to keep warm.
You might see them in the morning.
If you watch,
soon the butterflies will open their wings
and fly away, one by one.

The next night they fill another tree,
a little farther south,
and the next night another,
a little farther south,
until finally the monarch butterflies
reach their home for the winter.

ONE-WAY TRIP

No one knows why they do it,
but there are some little animals, called lemmings,
that go out and drown themselves.

Maybe they do it because they can't find enough food.
Maybe they do it because their homes are too crowded.
Maybe they do it because there are too many lemmings.
Or maybe the lemmings are sick.

Whatever the reason,
they gather in large groups, every few years,
and march down to the sea from their mountain homes.
They cross fields, streams, ponds, and lakes
until they come to the edge of the water.
They plunge in and swim until they become tired.
Then they drown.
A few lemmings stay behind to raise new families.

Napping All Winter

When someone in your home takes a nap, it usually lasts for an hour or so, but the naps some animals take may last all season.

The woodchuck is one of the long nappers. In the fall, when food is hard to find, the woodchuck, sometimes called a ground hog, waddles into its hole in the ground. There it rolls up in a ball and begins its long winter's nap. If you could touch a woodchuck or blow into its ear, it wouldn't wake up! The woodchuck naps all winter.

Other animals nap all winter, too—animals such as snakes, turtles, dormice, squirrels, prairie dogs, badgers, bears, and bats. Winter nappers aren't really sleeping. We say they're hibernating.

Some animals, like certain kinds of frogs, take long naps in both winter and summer. Other animals, such as the snail and the lungfish, take long naps only during summer. Summer nappers aren't really sleeping, either. We say they're estivating.

Guarding Their Lives

Every animal can protect itself.
Some animals protect themselves by running fast.
   Others protect themselves
   by standing very still,
   or hiding, or
   pretending to be dead.
Some animals protect themselves with teeth or tusks,
   or with claws, or hoofs, or nails,
   or with horns or antlers.
Some animals protect themselves
with weapons that poison,
   or sting,
   or stick,
   or shock,
   or smell bad.
On the next pages you will read
how various animals protect themselves.

ANIMALS THAT SHOCK

THE ELECTRIC EEL

Did you ever get an electric shock when you touched a doorknob after walking on a fuzzy carpet?

Fish that swim too near an electric eel get the same kind of shock. An electric eel makes electricity inside its body. One kind of electric eel that lives in the lakes and rivers of South America makes electricity strong enough to light a neon sign and strong enough to knock out a horse.

When enemy fish are around, the electric eel sends out small shocks which warn the enemy not to come any closer. Most fish dart away. But if a fish should come too close, the eel wiggles its muscles to send out a shock powerful enough to kill the animal.

AND STING

THE PORTUGUESE MAN-OF-WAR

When you see a Portuguese man-of-war, it looks like a blue balloon floating on the water. But don't go near it!

Under the "balloon" are long, stinging threads that hang far down into the water. The threads are filled with a stinging poison that helps to protect the Portuguese man-of-war.

If a small fish swims into these threads, it gets stung and captured for food. If a larger sea animal, such as an octopus, touches the threads, it gets stung, too. Then the large animal is frightened away, or it dies.

Hiding from enemies

THE CHAMELEON

The skin of a chameleon changes color faster than you can change your clothes. And sometimes this quick change of color saves the chameleon's life.

Snakes like to eat chameleons, but they can't always see them. When the chameleon sits on a tree limb, sometimes it looks brown—just like the limb.

But when it sits on a green leaf, the color of the chameleon is green.

But if the chameleon gets too cold or too warm, it may change to a color that doesn't hide it at all. Then it is easy for a snake to catch it.

THE SQUID

Some animals don't hide themselves—they hide their enemies. That's what a sea animal called the squid does.

Big fish like to eat squid. But just as the big fish gets close, the squid squirts an inky liquid at the fish. This inky liquid makes the water so black that the fish can't see the squid. By the time the water clears, the squid is far away and safe.

Octopuses also protect themselves by squirting a cloud of inky liquid. Squids and octopuses store the liquid inside their bodies—where it is always ready for use.

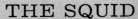

181

Guy Coheleach

HORNS AND ANTLERS

ANTLERS

When a deer is attacked, all it has to do is lower its head.
Its antlers become a wall of pointed branches.
Any animal, such as a wolf, that dares to attack a deer
is likely to be hurt by the deer's antlers.

But the deer has to keep out of sight in the spring
because late in winter its antlers fall off,
and the deer can't protect itself
until its new antlers are hard.

New antlers grow fast, though, and by fall the deer may have
even larger antlers than the ones it had the year before.
Then the deer comes out of hiding,
ready to protect itself against its enemies.

HORNS

The mountain goat has horns that never fall off.
If this goat is attacked by a mountain lion,
it will fight with its strong horns.

THE HORN THAT'S NOT A HORN

The horns of a rhinoceros are different from other animal horns.
They are made of something like hair or fingernails stuck together.
Yet the fierce rhinoceros can kill a lion
or knock over an automobile
by a charge with its boneless horns.

Teeth and Tusks

THE TIGER

Tigers have the same number of teeth as you do,
but their teeth are different from yours.
All their teeth are pointed
and as sharp as nails.
The tiger can kill
with one slash of its long teeth.
Other animals also use their teeth
to protect themselves,
but few have teeth as sharp as a tiger.

THE WART HOG

The wart hog's tusks are really teeth
that are too long to fit into its mouth.
When the wart hog is attacked by a leopard,
it can protect its face with its tusks,
but it still cannot protect its back and tail.
So the wart hog runs for its hole.
Then it whirls around and backs into the hole.
Now only its long tusks face the leopard,
and usually the leopard goes away.

Claws, Hoofs, and Nails

The feet of some animals have claws or nails as sharp as knives. Other animals have hoofs as hard as hammers. These animals use their claws, hoofs, or nails as weapons to protect themselves.

CATS

Have you ever seen a cat's claws? Sometimes you see them, sometimes you don't. But all cats—lions, tigers, leopards, even house cats—have long, curved claws.

Most of the time cats hide their claws in their paws. But when a cat is attacked by some other animal, it sticks out its claws and digs deep into the other animal's skin. The harder the animal struggles to get away, the deeper the cat's claws sink into it.

THE ZEBRA

A few hard kicks from a zebra
can drive away the hungriest jackal.
The zebra is a fierce fighter.
When the zebra is attacked,
it can kick forward and backward
with its hard hind hoofs
and bite with its teeth.

THE OSTRICH

The ostrich can't fly
even though it is a bird.
It has strong, sharp nails
on its feet for protection.
When the ostrich
is attacked,
it kicks forward
and downward
with its long,
powerful legs.
One hard, slashing kick
from the ostrich
can hurt an animal
as large as a horse.

SMELLS THAT PROTECT

THE SKUNK

Skunks can't run fast.
They don't have hoofs to kick with
or sharp horns to fight with.
But they can protect themselves by spraying a smelly liquid.

If a dog attacks a skunk,
it turns its back to the dog,
raises its bushy tail,
stamps its front feet,
and squirts the bad-smelling liquid
into the eyes and mouth of the dog.

The liquid makes the dog's eyes sting.
And the smell makes the dog run away as fast as it can.
The skunk strolls off
as if nothing had happened.

SKUNK CABBAGE

Skunk cabbage gets its name because it has a strong smell like that of a skunk. It has such a strong smell that no animal will eat it. If a hungry cow starts to nibble on this plant, the smell makes her snort and walk away.

Some birds and lizards even live under this smelly plant so that their enemies won't come near them.

Quills and Spines

THE PORCUPINE

The porcupine's quills are really stiff hairs.
Some people think porcupines shoot their quills, but they don't.

When a porcupine is attacked by a dog,
the porcupine shakes all over, rattling its quills.
The quills fall out easily,
and the barbed ends stick into the dog.
The dog runs away and leaves the porcupine alone.

The ends of the quills are like fishhooks—
they work themselves deeper and deeper into the skin.
This makes them harder to pull out.

THE "JUMPING" CACTUS

The "jumping" cactus,
or jumping cholla,
has sharp spines that protect it
from hungry desert animals.
The spines don't really jump,
but when the wind blows,
these spines fall from the cactus
and cover the ground.
They seem to "jump" into any animal
that happens to walk by.

These spines have barbed ends—
like the porcupine's quills.
Few animals come near
the "jumping" cactus a second time.

PAUL McNEAR

191

Animals that wear armor

THE ARMADILLO

The armadillo wears a suit of armor that is jointed like knights' armor of long ago. It is covered with bands of bone. It can roll into a ball when danger threatens.

If a bobcat comes near the armadillo, the armadillo tucks its head and feet under its body and covers them with its bands of thick skin. Then the armadillo is so round that the bobcat can't pick it up. Its skin is so tough that the bobcat can't tear it or bite through it.

THE BOX TURTLE

The shell of a box turtle is also something like a suit of armor. The box turtle can't roll into a ball, but sometimes it looks like one. It has a bony top shell like any other turtle, but its bottom shell has two parts connected by a hinge.

If a dog comes near, the turtle pulls its head, legs, and tail inside and clamps the hinge shut like a box to close the edges of its two shells.

Then the dog may toss the turtle in the air, bite it, scratch it, or even drag it home—without hurting the turtle at all.

ANIMALS
HARD TO SEE

There are animals
that can stand in the open
and still be hidden from their enemies.
See if you can find ten hidden animals
in this forest picture.

1. White-tailed deer
2. Fawn
3. Quail
4. Land turtle
5. Ground squirrel
6. Red fox
7. Sparrow
8. Snake
9. Moth
10. Tree frog

Animal Tricks

THE "PLAYING POSSUM" TRICK

The opossum often seems to "play dead" to save its life.

Suppose a hunting dog attacks an opossum. If the opossum can't get away, it will fall over in a faint and appear to be dead. It will lie with its mouth open, and its body will be as limp as a rag doll. If the dog bites the opossum or shakes it by the neck and tosses it in the air, the opossum will not make a sound.

When the dog finally leaves it for dead, the opossum "wakes up" and goes on its way.

THE "BROKEN WING" TRICK

The mother killdeer has a trick she often uses to protect her chicks.

Suppose a hungry cat comes near her nest on the ground. The mother killdeer pretends to have a broken wing and will flutter off and squawk loudly as if she were hurt. She makes so much noise that the cat begins to chase her. The mother killdeer flops in the air and drags one wing—always just ahead of the cat.

Soon she has led the cat far from her chicks. Then she flaps her wings and rises in the air. Her chicks are safe! She has tricked the cat.

SPEED FOR PROTECTION

The only way some animals can protect themselves is to run faster than their enemies.

THE GAZELLE

Lions would have gazelle for dinner every night if the gazelles were not such fast runners. But the gazelle is an antelope that can run faster than most birds can fly.

A lion can run fast, too, but only for a little while. The gazelle can run fast for a long time. It speeds across the plain, leaving the lion far behind.

THE RABBIT

Rabbits stay alive by running, too. But they have a special way of running. When a fox chases a rabbit, the rabbit zigzags. It runs first in one direction, then in another. It hops over bushes, around trees, behind stones.

The fox can run as fast as the rabbit. But the rabbit turns corners so quickly that the fox can't catch it.

Other animals that protect themselves by running fast are giraffes, white-tailed deer, antelopes, and mice.

199

Animal Warnings

THE BEAVER GUARD

As a family of beavers works, one of them will act as a guard.
The beaver on guard does not blow a whistle—it whacks its tail.

While the other beavers are busy building dams
or gathering food, the beaver guard watches and listens.
If it hears a strange noise, the beaver guard jumps into the pond.
Whack! Whack! Whack!   It slaps its broad tail on the water.

All the beavers stop work and dive into the water.
They swim as fast as they can until they reach their home
in the middle of the pond.
The beaver guard usually warns them in time to escape.

ANIMALS THAT WARN OTHERS

Some animals give danger warnings
not only to their own families,
but also to other animals.
A tiny antelope called the dik-dik
warns all animals nearby
with its shrill cries.

The tickbird warns the rhinoceros
of approaching danger.
It rides on the back
of the rhinoceros.
When it flaps its wings
and makes loud squawks,
the rhinoceros knows
that danger is near.

POISONS FOR PROTECTION

THE WHITE-FACED HORNET

Hum-m-m-m! hum-m-m-m! hum-m-m-m!
A hornet is building a nest.
It's so busy that
it doesn't see a small boy nearby.
CRASH!!!

A stone tears through the nest.
The hornet flies straight at the boy who threw it.
The hornet circles around and around.
Its wings make a loud, humming sound.
The boy slaps at it,
but this just makes the hornet mad.
This is where we get the phrase "mad as a hornet."

Suddenly, the hornet jabs its stinger into the boy's arm
and squirts out poison.
The hornet flies away to repair its nest,
leaving the boy with a big, red, swollen bump.
A hornet never stings
unless it is disturbed.

THE TOAD

Toads taste bad.
Because of this, other animals won't eat them.
Warts all over the back and the head of the toad
are filled with a poisonous fluid.

When toads are attacked,
their warts ooze enough poison
to make the attacking animal sick.
The poison gets into the mouth or nose of the animal
and makes it cough and sneeze.
Then the toad can hop away.

Some people think that you'll get warts if you touch toads.
But you won't!
The warts just protect the toad.

Living Together

When people live and work together,
we call them a family, a group, or a community.
When many of the same kinds of animals
or plants live together,
we call them
a flock of sheep,
or a school of fish,
or a herd of buffaloes,
or a pack of wolves.

When quails fly together,
we call them a covey of quail.
Dolphins swim together in groups called schools.
Geese fly overhead in a flock,
but we call them a gaggle of geese
when they land on water.

Seals gather together in harems.
Bananas grow in bunches.
And when trees grow in clumps,
we call them a grove,
or a copse, or a woods, or a forest.
It all depends on the size of the clump.

When animals or plants live together,
they help each other in many ways.
The next pages will show you how.

ANIMAL PLAYGROUNDS

Baby baboons play in a playground.
It is not a place with swings
and slides and monkeybars.
But it's a place where grown-up baboons
can watch baby baboons as they
shriek and chase one another around,
or grunt and wrestle in clouds of dust,
or pull one another's tails,
or smack one another on the back,
or tease and chase a giraffe,
or just walk around picking up sticks and stones,

or getting in the way of a passing elephant.
If the wrestling and the hitting get too rough,
or if a baby baboon is hurt and begins to howl,
the grown-up baboons will rush up to stop the play.

Young emperor penguins have playgrounds, too.
They stand in huddles like football players,
or take rides on floating cakes of ice,
or go swimming together.
But wherever young penguins play,
the grown-up penguins are always watching.

WOLVES HAVE A HUNTING POW-WOW

Wolf packs sometimes have pow-wows,
like Indians used to do, before they go hunting.
If you were hidden nearby,
this is what you might see.

A lone wolf lifts its shaggy head,
and howls a long low *a-r-r-o-o-o-o-o-o-o-o-w*.
The howl echoes through the dark and silent woods.
Again and again the great wolf howls.
Soon some shadowy shapes come loping toward him.
These are the other wolves in the wolf pack joining their leader.
After all the pack has gathered,
the wolves begin their pow-wow.
No one knows exactly why they have a pow-wow,
but they often do.

First, the great wolf raises its head and howls.
Another joins in, then another, and another,
until all the wolves are howling together.

Then suddenly they are silent.
Then they are gone—following their leader on the hunt.
If you could go with them, you would see them join
for another pow-wow after the hunt is over.
Again no one knows why.

BUSY MAKING HONEY

A beehive is a busy place, full of buzz and bustle and forty thousand bees, or more, busily making honey.

Some bees are making honey, and some bees are making wax rooms to store it in. Some bees are baby bees, some bees are taking care of the baby bees, and some bees are making food, called "beebread," for the baby bees. Some bees are lazy and are just sitting and buzzing while other bees are feeding them honey. Some bees are flying from flower to flower, gathering nectar to make the honey, and some bees are flying just for fun and practice. Some bees are fanning their wings to keep the hive cool. Some bees are even fighting robber bees that are trying to steal the honey in the hive.

Right in the middle of all this buzzing and bustling sits the biggest bee of all—the queen bee! And some bees are doing nothing but washing, combing, and feeding the queen! The queen does nothing but lay one egg after another to keep the hive alive with golden honeybees.

A ROOF-RAISING PARTY

You may have heard of
a "roof-raising" party
where people get together to help
a neighbor build a roof over his barn.

One kind of bird,
called a sociable weaverbird,
has "roof-raising" parties, too.
The weaverbirds get together
and build one big roof
that hangs in a tree.
The roof looks something like a tent.
The weaverbirds fly
and flutter here and there
in search of
sticks and straw,
and feathers and fur,
which they stick,
tuck, push, pull,
lace, weave, and twist,
until little by little, and stick by stick,
the birds have made a roof.
Then each weaverbird family
builds its own nest
under the one big roof.

Other birds do things together, too.
Penguins go fishing together.
Crows take turns at being lookout.
Some birds, called apostle birds,
live and work together
in groups of twelve—
seldom more and seldom less.

Some weaverbirds build small nests.

crows

Amazing Ants

Tiny ants live together, work together, and do some of the things that people do.

FARMER ANTS

Some ants plant crops and grow their food somewhat as farmers do. First, the ants munch on leaves until the leaves become mushy. Then they store the mush in little rooms inside their home. They plant mushroom spores on the munched-up leaves. In time the mushrooms grow and become food for the ants.

ANTS THAT KEEP DAIRIES

Some ants have dairy farms. But instead of milking real cows, they milk little insects called aphids. Instead of herding them to pasture, the ants carry their "cows" from place to place.

ANTS THAT BUILD BRIDGES

Some ants build bridges. Army ants spend most of their lives scurrying and scuttling over the ground in huge swarms. If they come to a stream, some of the ants make a bridge of themselves by holding each other's legs to make a chain. Then the rest of the ants cross on the backs of those that made the bridge.

THE ANTS' HONEY FOUNTAIN

Some ants store food for others. They stuff themselves with honey until they are as round as peas. Then they spend the rest of their lives as living honeypots hanging from the top of a tunnel. Hungry ants that pass beneath them reach up to get a drink of honey.

worker ants with larvae

WALLS OF ANTLERS, HOOFS, AND HORNS

Some animals can't build walls of wood or stone.
But some herds of animals line up
in rings or squares
and make a wall with their bodies, antlers, hoofs, or horns.
This kind of wall protects the others in the herd.

A WALL OF ANTLERS

Reindeer herds sometimes make a wall of antlers
to protect themselves from packs of hungry wolves.
When the wolves try to sneak near,
the reindeer bunch tightly together,
with the weak animals on the inside
and the strong ones on the outside.

Then, lowering their antlers,
the strong reindeer gallop in a ring around the herd.
Soon the rest of the herd is running and milling
around and around
inside the galloping ring of reindeer,
whose mighty antlers form a whirling wall.
When the wolves cannot get past the whirling antlers,
they slink away.

A WALL OF HOOFS AND HORNS

Musk oxen herds protect themselves from wolves
by standing in a ring.
If a herd is attacked,
the fathers stand side by side and make a circle
around the mothers and young.
Their tossing horns
and slashing hoofs form a wall that keeps out prowling wolves.

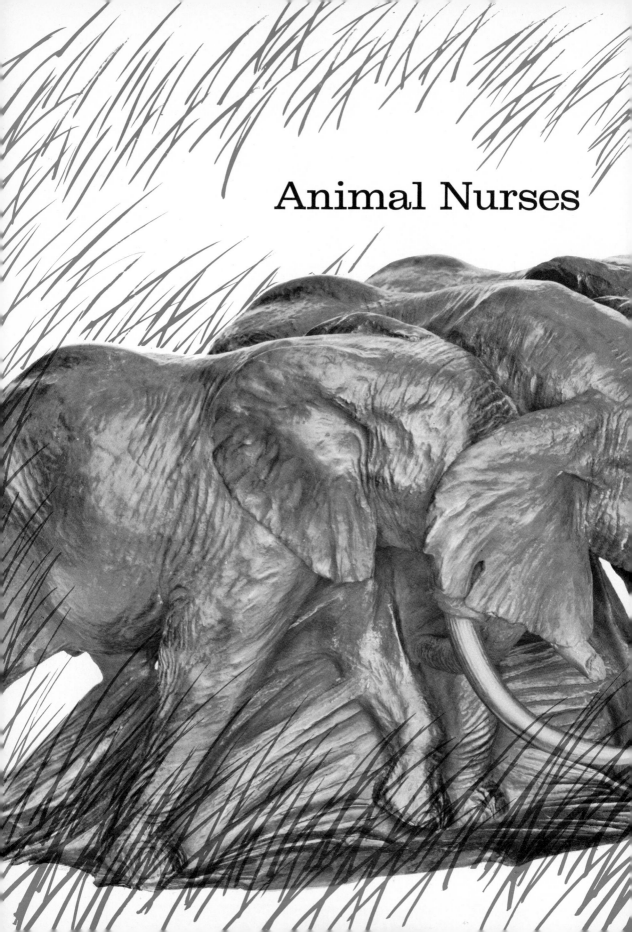

Animal Nurses

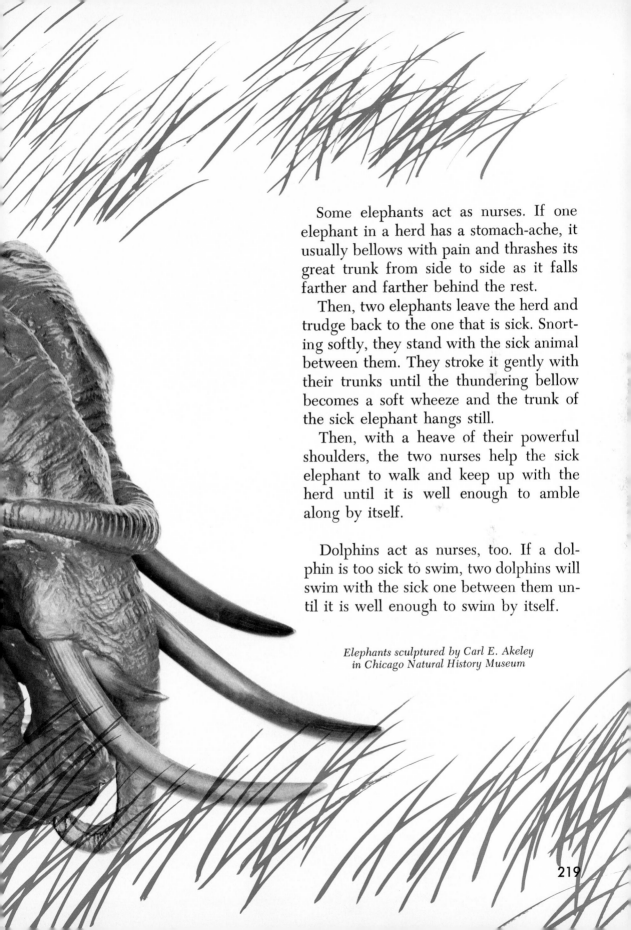

Some elephants act as nurses. If one elephant in a herd has a stomach-ache, it usually bellows with pain and thrashes its great trunk from side to side as it falls farther and farther behind the rest.

Then, two elephants leave the herd and trudge back to the one that is sick. Snorting softly, they stand with the sick animal between them. They stroke it gently with their trunks until the thundering bellow becomes a soft wheeze and the trunk of the sick elephant hangs still.

Then, with a heave of their powerful shoulders, the two nurses help the sick elephant to walk and keep up with the herd until it is well enough to amble along by itself.

Dolphins act as nurses, too. If a dolphin is too sick to swim, two dolphins will swim with the sick one between them until it is well enough to swim by itself.

Elephants sculptured by Carl E. Akeley in Chicago Natural History Museum

ROCK CASTLES
UNDER THE SEA

Who builds rock castles under the sea?
One animal, called a coral polyp, makes the rocks.
It is like a brickmaker.
Another creature, called an alga, cements the rocks together.
It is like a plasterer.

The coral polyp looks like a flower with many petals
as it sits and eats food at the bottom of the sea.
Inside the body of the polyp,
the food is made into tiny rocks.
And as the rocks are made,
the alga covers them and joins them with pink cement
that the alga makes inside its body.

The tiny rocks spread
and spiral up and up
making a craggy castle filled with
hundreds of holes, halls, and secret passages
through which brightly colored fish dart and swim.

Sometimes the castle gets so high that
the sea no longer covers it,
and a coral island is born.

Plants that
live together

A lichen looks like one plant, but it is really two. The part of the lichen you can see is called the fungus. It can't live without the other part, called an alga. But the alga, which lives inside the fungus, can live separately.

Lichens sometimes hang in strands from old logs or stand in tiny clumps on a rock. The alga makes the food that feeds the fungus. The fungus protects the alga from drying up in the sun or from being blown away by the wind.

The fungus and the alga live together and help each other live. So the lichen doesn't need many of the parts that other plants have. It doesn't need roots to get food from the ground, and it doesn't need leaves to store the food. Lichens can just sit on a rock and grow.

Moss looks like one plant, but it is really thousands growing together. Each tiny moss plant is so tangled with the others that together they are one matted clump.

moss

lichen

Queer, Quaint, and Curious

What would you think if someone told you
about an insect called *no-see-ums midge,*
or animals called *sassaby* and *shou?*

What would you think about
a bean that jumps
or a monkey's face
that is red, white, and blue?

And what would you think if someone told you
about a worm that looks like a feather duster
or a fish that blows itself up like a balloon?

You might think it queer,
or quaint,
or you might think it curious.
But all these creatures,
and many more just as odd
live in the world around you.

NAMES THAT ARE FUN

The names of many plants and animals are often fun to say.
Some animal names are
aye-aye, bongo,
bush baby, puku,
numbat, sassaby, shou—
potoroo, wallaroo, wapiti, wallaby,
softly-softly, squeaker.
There is even a monkey
that people call a monkey-monkey monkey.

One fish is called a Hippoglossus hippoglossus,
while others are called
scat, scup, snook,
silver dollar, snaggle tooth,
lookdown, puffer, and grunt.

Birds may have names like
go-away and noddy,
or sooty oyster catcher,
or kokako, kittiwake,
and ula-ai-hawane.

Insects have funny names, too,
like ball roller, bessy bug,
fairy fly, and hu-hu beetle—
or doodlebug, tumblebug,
sticktight flea, and no-see-ums midge.

Dutchman's-breeches
and shooting star are names of flowers.
And have you ever heard of a cannon-ball tree
or a cucumber tree?

cucumber tree

ball roller

sooty oyster catcher

silver dollar

bush baby

TO SAY

doodlebug

Dutchman's-breeches

scat

aye-aye

lookdown

kittiwake

puku

shooting stars

ula-ai-hawane

227

Feather-Duster Worm

Not all worms are fat, brown, and wriggly like the ones you use for fishing. Some worms look like feather dusters!

A feather-duster worm digs its tail deep into the sand at the bottom of the sea. As it digs, it builds a papery tube around itself. Then the feather-duster worm lies in the tube with its feathery end sticking out of the sand. If something scares the worm, it pulls in its feathery end and slithers down the tube to hide.

feather-duster worm

PADDLE WORMS AND FLATWORMS

Another kind of worm, called a chainworm, swims through water by waving a row of tiny paddles along each side of its body.

Some worms that are flat tumble across the sand at the bottom of the sea like autumn leaves tossed by a wind.

Some worms lie in a pile on a leaf and look like a tangle of bright-red ribbon. There are worms that look like shoelaces and others that seem to tie themselves in knots.

ribbon worm

flatworm

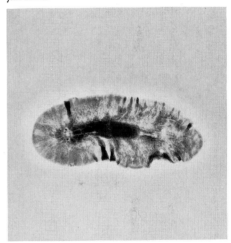

bootlace worm

229

The Secret of
the Jumping Bean

Why does a "jumping bean" jump?
What makes it tumble
and hop over the ground?
The "bean" itself doesn't jump,
but a little animal inside it does.
The animal is a baby moth
that grows up inside the "bean."

When the sun makes the ground hot,
the tiny moth gets too warm.
So it hooks its legs into the "bean"
and twists
and jerks its tiny body with all its might.
And when the baby moth jerks,
the "bean" jumps—*plip, plip, plip, plip*—
until it hops into a cool spot.

Then the "bean" cools off,
and the baby moth stops jerking.
When the baby moth stops jerking,
the "bean" stops jumping.

Animals with funny faces

Clowns paint their faces red, white, and blue.
But faces are funny on animals, too!

An animal face can be
spotted,
or striped,
or red, white, and blue.
It can be furry,
or feathery,
or hidden by hair.

An animal face can be wrinkled
or smooth.
It can be covered with horns
or plated with armor.

An animal face can be bumpy
or warty.
An animal can have a beard
or bulging eyes,
or it can have a tuft on top of its head
and a ruff around its face.

AN ANIMAL ACROBAT

Tree frogs are acrobats.

The tips of their fingers and toes are like suction cups.
Wherever a tree frog puts its fingers and toes,
they stick
until the frog decides to move.

A tree frog, sitting on the stem of a river reed,
can suddenly leap into a tree
and hang from a twig by one of its toes.

Then it can spring from the twig,
catch a moth in mid-air,
and land with a plop on a swaying leaf.

A tree frog can walk upside down
like a fly on a ceiling, too.
It can run headfirst down a tree trunk,
or it can leap to a stem on a nearby bush.
It can even swing from twig to twig in a tree
like an acrobat on a flying trapeze.

A HUFF AND A PUFF

You can huff and puff to blow up a balloon.
But some animals can blow up their noses, or
throats, or even their whole bodies.

A NOSE IN THE AIR

If someone disturbs a sleeping elephant seal,
it wakes up with a bellow. It huffs and puffs
to blow up its nose until the nose sticks up in
the air. Then, gurgling and bellowing, the
bright-pink seal waddles away.

A BAG OF AIR TO SING WITH

One kind of toad huffs and puffs to fill its
body with air. Just when it seems as though
its body might burst, the toad lets the air out
in a sudden long *c-r-o-o-a-k.*

PLAYING CATCH WITH A FISH

You could play catch with a puffer fish, which
puffs itself into a ball. When it is pulled from
the sea, a puffer fish fills itself with air. If you
throw the fish back into the sea, it will bob on
the water until the air leaks out of its mouth.
When the air is gone, the fish sinks and swims
away.

Saving What We Have

Imagine what would happen
if people had no water to drink,
no soil to grow food,
no trees for wood to build houses.
Water, soil, and trees
are some of our natural resources—
gifts of nature that people need to live.
It's important to use natural resources wisely—
to conserve them—
so there will always be enough of them.
On the next few pages, you can learn something about
conserving our natural resources.

SAVING THE SOIL

Mighty windstorms can pick up and blow away tons of soil from a farmer's land.

Heavy rainstorms can run down hills and wash away more tons of soil.

Without soil, farmers can't grow crops for food. How can farmers protect, or conserve, soil from windstorms and rainstorms?

One way they can protect the soil is by *strip cropping*. *Strip cropping* means planting different kinds of crops side by side—in strips. One of the crops is usually of a kind that grows thick and close together—such as hay or grass. The thick-growing crop helps to catch the wind and slow it down so it won't blow away the soil.

Another way farmers can protect soil is by *contour farming*. *Contour farming* means planting crops in rows that wind or curve according to the shape, or contour, of the land.

Instead of plowing hilly land up and down the hill, the farmers plow across the hill. Every furrow that the plows make acts as a tiny dam that catches water. Then rainwater will seep into the ground and help crops grow, instead of flowing down the hill and washing away the soil.

Strip cropping and *contour farming* are just a few of the tricks that farmers use to protect the soil from rainstorms and wind-storms.

New Mexico—1936 *by Charles Edmondson for the Field Enterprises Educational Corporation collection*

whooping crane

mountain sheep

petrel

KEEPING ANIMALS FROM DYING OUT

Nobody knows what dinosaurs were really like. Of course, scientists can make some pretty good guesses. They can even build model dinosaurs for museums. But nobody—not even the smartest scientist—knows for sure what a living, breathing, eating, stomping dinosaur was really like. Dinosaurs died out long ago—long before anybody could see them.

What happened to dinosaurs almost happened to buffaloes. And it almost happened to many other kinds of wildlife—puffins, petrels, pelicans, trumpeter swans, antelope, mountain sheep, black-tailed deer, white-tailed deer, geese, ducks, pheasants, herons, and whooping cranes. And those are only a few.

Fewer and fewer of these animals were staying alive. Hunters were shooting them. Other animals were attacking them. Diseases were destroying them.

Horicon Marsh, in Wisconsin, is one of the many game refuges in the United States.

But some men realized that many people don't want to see these animals die out. People don't want to see these animals stuffed and still in some museum. They want to see what these animals are really like, living in the prairies, the marshes, and the forests. So, the men helped to set up special places, called *wildlife refuges,* where the animals would be protected from enemies and diseases.

Wildlife refuges have helped to keep these animals from dying out. And they have helped us to know what the animals are really like.

WATCHING THE WATER

The word *reservoir* comes from an Old French word
that means "to reserve," or "save."
When we use the word *reservoir,*
we usually mean
    either the place where we keep water in reserve
    or the water itself that we keep in reserve.

Many people have to keep a reserve, or *reservoir,* of water,
especially in places where there isn't a lot of rain.
Without the reservoir, people might not have water for
    drinking
    or washing
    or growing crops
    or making power to produce electricity.

Some people, when they go on a hike,
reserve water in canteens.
The canteens are reservoirs.
Many people reserve rain water in barrels
next to their back doors.
The rainbarrels are reservoirs.
Many people on the island of Bermuda
reserve rain water in storage tanks
that are part of their houses.
The storage tanks are reservoirs.
Factories, towns, and small cities
often have water reserved in huge water towers.
The water towers are reservoirs.

In many areas where there are lots of people
who use millions of gallons of water every day,
water is reserved in lake-like reservoirs.
These reservoirs are reservoirs.

lake reservoir

storage tank reservoir in Bermuda

water tower reservoir

HELPING
TO PROTECT
THE FORESTS

Are you tired of hearing these warnings?
• Don't play with matches.
• Make sure you've completely extinguished the campfire.
• Only you can prevent forest fires.
Maybe you are, but there are good reasons
for these warnings and reminders.

Look around you!
Where does the wood on the floor come from? Trees!
Where does the wood in your desk and chair come from? Trees!
Where does the wood in your pencil come from? Trees!
Where does the paper in this book come from? Trees!
That's hardly a start on the list of things
that forests supply for our needs.

If you were to plant a tree today,
it would take years for that tree to grow
big enough so it could be chopped down and used as lumber.
But a forest fire could wipe out acres and acres of such trees
in just a few hours.
In fact, forest fires destroy about 3,000,000 acres
of forest every year—
and that's only in the United States.

Now, maybe these statements make more sense:
• Don't play with matches.
• Make sure you've completely extinguished the campfire.
• Only you can prevent forest fires.

SAVING WHAT WE CAN'T REPLACE

The trouble with metals is
that they come from minerals.
And the trouble with minerals is
that they have no life.
Minerals can't grow again and replace themselves
as can cotton and cabbage, carrots and corn.

If we don't conserve, or save, minerals, we won't have
    any lead for pipes,
    any copper for telephone wires,
    any iron and steel for automobiles.

But there are some ways that minerals can be conserved.
    Things made with minerals can be used over again
    after they have been thrown away as junk.
        Minerals can't grow again.

    Things can be made with substitutes
    for minerals that are scarce.
        Minerals can't grow again.

    Other things can be made with scraps
    and leftovers of minerals
    so nothing is wasted.
        Minerals can't grow again.

Minnesota iron ore mine on the Mesabi range

PLACES TO PLAY

National parks are large plots of land
that have mountains or canyons or swamps
or lakes or forests or beaches.
Some national parks have many of these attractions.
National parks are set aside by the government
to conserve the beauty of nature
and to conserve space
for places where
people can visit and enjoy themselves.
In a national park, people may go
hiking or camping
or swimming or boating
or just plain sightseeing.

Rocky Mountain National Park, Colorado

Banff National Park, Alberta, Canada

Everglades National Park, Florida

Yosemite National Park, California

Acadia National Park, Maine

Mammoth Cave National Park, Kentucky

Living on a Farm

If you live on a farm,
you find out many things
about plants and animals
as you take care of them
and watch them grow.

Here are some of the things
you may find out:
A tomato is really a big berry.
Ducks have waterproof feathers.
A pig is smarter than you think.
Cows have four parts to their stomachs
Apple buds wear furry coats in the wintertime.
A male turkey has a "beard" of feathers on its chest.
Goslings shouldn't go near the water
for the first few weeks.

On farms in other lands, you might find
different kinds of plants and animals:
Water buffaloes instead of horses in China
Papayas instead of apples in the Pacific islands
Ostriches instead of chickens in Africa
Yaks instead of cows in Tibet.
On the next pages you can find out
more about the animals and plants on farms.

WHY HORSES WEAR SHOES

If you walk barefoot on rocks and pebbles and rough, hard ground, your feet will get cut and bruised. So you wear shoes to protect your feet.

A work horse's feet are different from yours. A horse walks on tough, thick hoofs that are really blunt toenails. They are as hard as the horns of a cow.

A work horse needs shoes even though its hoofs are tough and thick. A work horse pulls heavy loads over rocks and pebbles and rough, hard ground. Without shoes, the hoofs of the work horse would split on the rocky roads.

254

Horseshoes don't look like your shoes, but they have to fit the horse's hoofs, just as your shoes have to fit your feet. Special pieces of iron are bent and fitted to each of the horse's four hoofs. Nails hold each iron shoe on. The nails which go into the horny hoof don't hurt the horse because the horse cannot feel them.

Cowboys' horses are different. Sometimes they do not need shoes if they run only on grassland or on soft sand, instead of on rough, rocky roads.

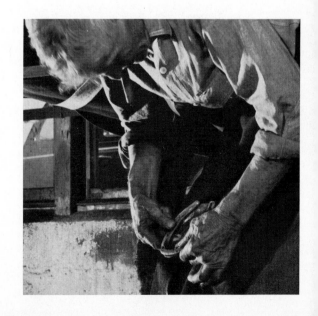

WHEN DOES A COW GIVE MILK?

If you tried to drink all the milk
that a good milk cow gives,
you would have to drink forty-four glasses of milk each day.
But cows don't always give milk.
A cow doesn't give milk until she is at least two years old
and has had a calf.
Then the cow gives milk for about a year.
After that, the milk supply dries up,
and the cow has to have another calf
before she can give milk again.

Some kinds of cows give more milk than others.
Cows called Holsteins give the most milk of all,
but their milk isn't very creamy.
Cows called Jerseys and Guernseys give creamy milk,
but they don't give as much milk as Holsteins.

MILK FROM OTHER ANIMALS

In many parts of the world,
people drink milk from other animals.
In the mountains of Switzerland, Norway,
and Sweden, people drink milk from goats.
In the deserts of Arabia and Asia,
people drink milk from camels.
People in Tibet drink milk from yaks.
And in the cold lands of the Arctic,
people drink milk from reindeer.

Sheep need tender care

Wild sheep can take care of themselves,
but tame sheep can't.
When sheep are tame, they scare easily.
They bleat and scatter and sometimes run into danger.
So shepherds train sheep dogs to watch over them.
The sheep dog barks and snaps at the sheep
to keep them from falling behind.
And the dog scares wild animals away.

SHEEP GET THEIR TOENAILS TRIMMED

A sheep's hoofs are its toenails,
and they have to be trimmed just as yours do.
Farmers trim the hoofs of tame sheep
with shears and a pocketknife.
Trimming keeps the hoofs short and neat.
But wild sheep don't need to have their hoofs trimmed.
Their hoofs wear down
as they run over rocky mountains.

SHEEP GET WOOLCUTS

You get haircuts, but tame sheep get woolcuts.
Their wool is cut only once each spring,
when it is softest and fluffiest
and will make the best wool clothes.
The sheep don't get cold after a woolcut
because the summer is warm.
And more wool will grow by the time cold weather comes again.
Wild sheep never get woolcuts
because their coats don't make good wool clothes.

A RING IN ITS NOSE

Some people wear rings on their fingers, but a hog may wear a ring in its nose. Farmers put rings in the noses of hogs so the hogs won't use their flat, turned-up snouts to shovel out tunnels under fences to get away. The ring pinches the hog's nose when it tries to dig this way.

HOGS IN MANY SIZES AND COLORS

Hogs come in different sizes. A big, fat hog may weigh more than 1,000 pounds. But other kinds of full-grown hogs may weigh only 500 pounds. Hogs come in different colors, too. Small Yorkshire hogs are snowy white. Duroc hogs are brick red. Spotted Poland China hogs are black with white spots. Hampshire hogs are black except for a white streak around their shoulders and front legs.

THE TRUTH ABOUT HOGS

Some people think that hogs are dirty, greedy, stupid animals. But farmers know better. Hogs get dirty only because they want to keep cool by wallowing in mud. And hogs aren't greedy— they eat the kind of food that makes them fat, but they never eat more than they need. And hogs aren't stupid—they can even learn to push a lever in the barnyard to get a drink of water or a dish of food.

CALLING ALL HOGS

When some farmers want their hogs to come and eat, they give a loud, long, hog call—

"S O O O O O O O O O O U U U U U U U E E E E E Y Y Y Y y y y y Pig Pig Pig Pig Pig Pig Pig Pig!"

Hogs can hear this loud call when they are more than a half mile away.

Chickens lay an egg a day

An egg a day,
an egg a day—
that's more than *most* birds
ever lay.
But a chicken is a bird, and it can lay
an egg almost every day.
Most farmers keep chicken flocks,
so that they can have plenty of eggs to
eat and to sell.

FOOLING THE CHICKENS
In the fall when it gets dark early,
chickens fall asleep earlier.
When they are asleep, they can't lay eggs,
so the farmer fools them by
putting bright lights in the chicken coop.
The chickens think it is still daytime and stay awake.
Then they don't stop laying eggs.

BROWN AND WHITE EGGS

Some eggs are brown
and some are white.
But the insides of both
are just alike.
Only the color of the shell is different.
Certain kinds of chickens, such as
Leghorns and Minorcas,
always lay white eggs.
Other kinds of chickens, such as
Plymouth Rocks and Rhode Island Reds,
always lay brown eggs.
When many kinds of chickens are in the same flock,
the farmer gathers both brown and white eggs in his basket.

Leghorn chicken   Minorca chicken   Plymouth Rock chicken   Rhode Island Red chicken

MOTHERLESS CHICKS

Some little chicks never see their mother.
They hatch in a special warm box called an incubator.
Then the farmer puts them in a little house
called a brooder house.
If little chicks stayed with their mother
and other big chickens in the yard,
they might get sick from chickenyard lice and germs.
But brooder houses are warm and clean,
and the chicks are kept safe and healthy as they grow.

KEEPING TURKEYS OUT OF TROUBLE

Turkeys aren't as smart as most barnyard animals. They always seem to be doing things they shouldn't do. A turkey picks up and eats all kinds of dirty things from the ground. Then it gets sick. So turkey farmers cut off a part of each turkey's upper beak. This keeps the upper and lower points of the beak from snapping together. With a clipped beak, a turkey can't pick up things from the ground. It has to get its food from a safe, clean turkey feeder.

Turkeys don't even know enough to stay in their safe pens. Sometimes they fly over the fence and land on the other side where dangerous animals can get them. So turkey farmers clip the turkey's wing feathers to keep them from flying.

Turkeys get scared of dark shadows and noises on bright moonlit nights. So turkey pens need night lights to keep the turkeys from stampeding and getting hurt and bruised. The night lights are flares. They make the turkeys feel safe and also keep other animals away.

Corn and How It Grows

If you grew as fast as corn does,
you would grow to be taller than your father
in less than a week.
Corn grows three to five inches a day in the summer.
And when it stops growing,
it is usually taller than a man.

CORNSTALK RIDDLE

Do you know why TV antennas and cornstalks are alike?
Because they both need props to hold them up.
You have probably seen the slanting wires, called guy wires,
that people put on TV antennas
to hold them up.
Cornstalks grow their own props.
After the corn gets tall,
prop roots start growing out from the stalks,
a little above the ground.
The roots grow down and push into the earth.
They hold the stalks firm
so that big winds won't blow them down.

CORN OF MANY COLORS

Corn isn't always yellow.
The kernels of Indian corn, called maize,
are black, blue, red, and even pink.
Some kernels are big and some are little.
Some are as tiny as grains of rice,
and some are as big as quarters.

WHAT HAS BIG EARS AND CAN'T HEAR?

A kind of corn that grows in Mexico
has ears that are nearly as long
as a yardstick.
And the cornstalks are so big and thick
that people build fences with them.

ROOTS THAT CRACK THE EARTH

Farmers plant sweet clover because clover roots crack and break up hard ground. The clover plant looks delicate, but its roots are long and thick and tough. They grow far down into the ground, pushing and cracking the earth around them. Water and air can get down through the cracks to make the soil richer. Then other plants can grow well in the soil.

BLOSSOMS FOR THE BEES

Another reason farmers plant clover is that bees gather nectar from the clover blossoms. Then the farmer who has beehives will have plenty of honey for himself, and even some for you.

ANIMALS EAT CLOVER

Sweet clover tastes good to the horses, the cattle, and the hogs on a farm, too. So farmers let their animals graze in fields of clover in the spring.

LUCKY FOUR-LEAF CLOVER

Have you ever looked for a four-leaf clover among the many with three leaves? Some people think four-leaf clovers are "lucky." But they really aren't. They are just hard to find.

Roundup time on a Wyoming cattle ranch

KINDS OF FARMS

Old MacDonald had a farm with chickens, ducks,
turkeys, pigs, cows, sheep, and donkeys.
And he probably grew corn, oats, wheat,
barley, alfalfa, and clover.
But many farmers today grow just one or two crops,
and raise just one or two kinds of animals.

Farmers grow celery, lettuce, onions, and tomatoes
on *truck farms.*
Truck farms are like large vegetable gardens.

On *fruit farms,*
farmers grow avocados, grapefruit,
apples, oranges, and other fruits.

Farmers raise milk cows on *dairy farms.*
The farmers feed them and keep them healthy
so that the cows will give a steady supply of milk.
The milk that most people in cities drink
comes from dairy farms.

The chickens, turkeys, and ducks
sold in most grocery stores
come from *poultry farms.*
Poultry farmers raise
thousands of birds every year.

Most cattle and sheep are raised on *ranches.*
In Australia, sheep ranches are called *sheep stations.*
And more sheep are raised there than in any other country.

A sheep station in Australia

Out of the Ground

Plants can't move around on their own.
But they are living things.
   They eat.
   They drink.
   They grow.
   They change as they grow
   into many kinds of shapes and sizes.
   And most plants have seeds
   that become new plants.

Plants are interesting things.
   Some grow where you don't expect them.
   Some smell good.
   Some live in houses.
   Some have unusual names.
   Some are even dangerous.

On the next pages, you can find out
some facts about the living things
that grow out of the ground—plants.

UNDERGROUND SUPPORT

Could a mighty maple tree crash into the street
if you leaned against it?
Or could a huge oak tree topple
in a soft summer breeze?
They could—in fact, most trees would—
if they didn't have roots to hold them up.

The roots of a tree are like strong branches.
But, instead of stretching up and out in the air,
they grow down and out in the ground.
The roots of some trees grow out and out
until they spread as widely under the ground
as the branches spread.

As the roots grow and grow,
they anchor the tree more and more firmly to the ground.
The roots of many trees hold so firmly
that, in a powerful wind,
the trunk of the tree would snap or split
before the roots would pop out of the ground.
Roots also help to keep a tree alive.
They soak up moisture from the ground.
The rest of the tree needs that moisture to live.
Roots are one of the most important parts of a tree.
In fact, roots are one of the most important parts
of almost all plants.

This picture shows part of the root system
of a tree
that was uprooted by a tornado.

STEMS

How is the stem
of a big elm tree
like the stem
of a daisy?
They don't look alike.
The daisy stem
is green and skinny
and easy to twist and bend.
And the stem of the elm
is a thick dark trunk—
stiff and strong.

But the stems
of these plants—
in fact,
the stems of most plants—
are alike in some ways.

They hold the leaves
and blossoms and branches
up to the fresh air
and sunlight.

Inside the stems are special cells
that help to keep the plants alive.
They serve as pipelines
to carry water and minerals and food
up and down the stems
to the many growing parts of the plants.
Some of the cells, called *vessels* and *tracheids*,
carry water and minerals
soaked up from the ground by the roots.

Other cells, called *sieve tubes*,
carry food made in the leaves.
These special cells are located
throughout the stem.
Even a tiny part of the stem
has many cells for carrying
water and minerals and food.

The stem of a daisy and the stem of a tree
may not look alike.
But now you know how they are alike—
in some ways.

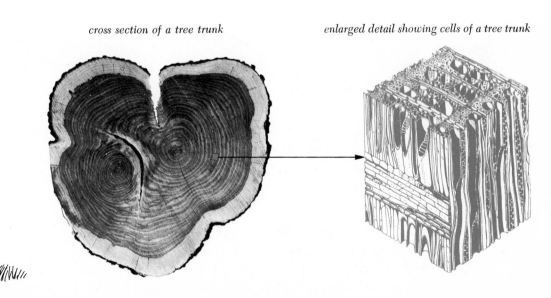

cross section of a tree trunk   *enlarged detail showing cells of a tree trunk*

LOTS OF LEAVES

When you think of leaves,
you might think of leaves from a maple tree,
an oak tree, or a chestnut tree.
But the shapes and sizes of some leaves
might surprise you.

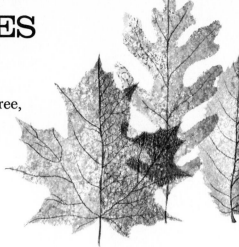

These leaves grow only about as long
as your little finger.
Each one is as narrow as a needle.
In fact, we call these leaves "needles."
They are leaves from a spruce tree.

You can cut off the tops of these leaves,
and the parts that are left can keep growing.
They are leaves of grass.

These leaves look like flower petals.
But the tiny yellow blossom in the center is the flower.
And the things that look like petals
are the white leaves of the flowering dogwood.

278

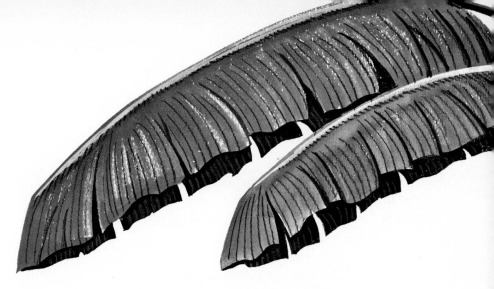

Some of these leaves grow so big
that just one could cover two bathtubs
placed end to end.
They are leaves from a banana tree.

And some of these leaves grow so big
that just one could cover the roof of a big truck.
They are leaves from an African raffia palm tree.

THE SWEET SMELL OF FLOWERS

Violets smell sweet.
So do roses and lilacs and honeysuckle vines.
Almost all flowers smell fresh and sweet.
That sweet smell, or fragrance, is important—
but not just for sniffing and enjoying.
The fragrance of flowers is important
to insects and birds—and to the flowers, as well.

For example, a bee that smells a fragrant flower
goes straight to it,
looking for nectar to make honey.
The bee picks up more than just the nectar.
As it pokes around inside the flower,
it also picks up powdery pollen grains
that stick to its body.

When the bee goes from that flower
to another one,
in search of more nectar,
it carries the pollen grains with it.
At the next flower,
some of the pollen grains rub off the bee
and get into a part of the flower called the *pistil*.
When pollen enters the pistil of a flower,
it helps to make seeds that can become new flowers.

The fragrance of flowers is pleasant to smell.
But, just as important, it helps
to attract insects and birds to the flowers.
And it helps the insects and birds
help flowers make more flowers.

WANDERING SEEDS

Before seeds can grow into new plants,
they have to leave the plants they grow on
and scatter to new growing ground.
But how do they get to the ground
where they're going to grow?
Different seeds travel in different ways.

Acorns fall from an oak tree
and bounce away.

Maple tree seeds have wings that spin
and ride in the air and carry them far away.

Dandelion seeds have a hairy parachute
that helps them float in the wind.

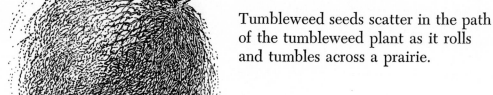

Tumbleweed seeds scatter in the path
of the tumbleweed plant as it rolls
and tumbles across a prairie.

Wild geranium seeds shoot through the air
from tiny seed cups
that snap loose, pop open, and curl up.

Burrs from sandburs stick to people's clothes and to animals' fur
and are dropped off or picked off somewhere else.

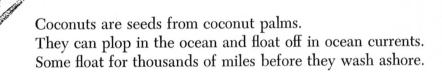

Coconuts are seeds from coconut palms.
They can plop in the ocean and float off in ocean currents.
Some float for thousands of miles before they wash ashore.

Corn kernels, like many other seeds,
are carried to new growing ground
by people and machines.

Seeds are wanderers.
They have to be, if they're going to get
where they're going to grow.

POISON PLANTS

If you eat or touch or sniff some plants,
they can make you sick.
Some poisonous plants can even kill you.

If you see mushrooms in a meadow
or under a tree, don't pick them.
Poisonous mushrooms look very much like good mushrooms.
But poisonous mushrooms have killed people
who have eaten them.
This picture shows what some poisonous mushrooms look like.

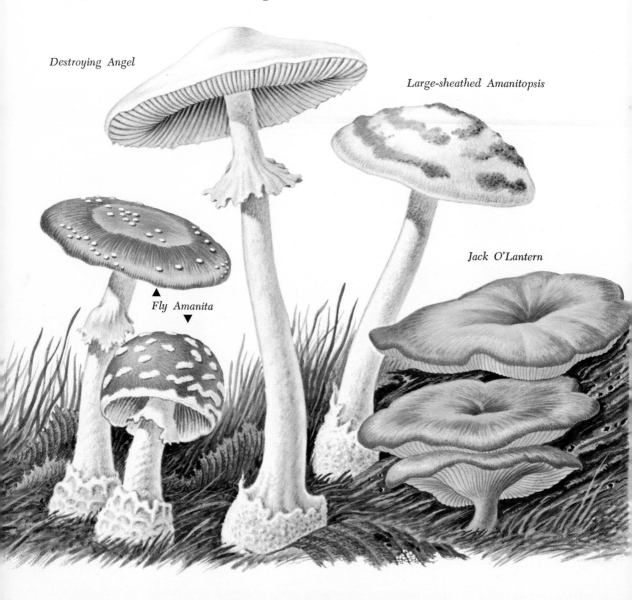

Destroying Angel

Large-sheathed Amanitopsis

Fly Amanita

Jack O'Lantern

If you walk through the woods,
you should never touch poison ivy.
It can make your skin itch and blister.

Many people are bothered when they sniff
the powdery pollen grains from ragweed.
They sneeze, and their eyes water and burn.
The ragweed pollen is a kind of poison to those people.

Those aren't the only poisonous plants.
Poisonous plants can grow anywhere
that other plants can grow.
So you should be careful not to eat or touch or sniff
plants that you don't recognize.

giant ragweed   *poison ivy*

HOUSES FOR FLOWERS AND PLANTS

Where can flowers and other plants
grow all year 'round—
even when the ground is white with snow?
In a greenhouse, that's where.

A greenhouse is a building
made mostly of glass or plastic.
It has glass or plastic roofs and walls
that let in just the right amount of sunlight.
It has windows on hinges
that let in just the right amount of fresh air.
It has water pipes and heating pipes
that give it just the right amount of water and heat.
A greenhouse gives flowers and other plants
just the right amount of everything they need to grow.

A greenhouse also protects the plants
from frost and snow and cold winds in the winter
and from hot, dry air or too much rain in the summer.
No matter what the weather is like outside,
it's always just right for the plants
inside a greenhouse.   286

WHEN IS A PLANT
A WEED?

If you really want your garden to grow,
one thing that you have to do is yank up the weeds.
A weed is any plant that grows in a garden or field
that isn't supposed to grow there.
You can yank up
pigweed, pokeweed, ragweed, milkweed,
quack grass, crab grass, thistles—even clover.

Clover is an important crop to farmers.
It makes feed for horses, cows, and other livestock.
And when some clover is plowed under the soil,
its chemicals help make the soil richer
and better for growing crops.

But suppose you're growing beans and carrots
and tomatoes and radishes in your garden.
And suppose you haven't planted *anything* else there,
and you don't want *anything* else to grow there.

Sometimes, clover grows wild
in gardens and fields and lawns.
If it grows in your garden,
and you don't want it to grow there,
it's a weed.
Yank it up!

FLOWERS THAT LOOK LIKE THEIR NAMES

Many kinds of flowers
have names that describe
what they look like.

Can you see how
the flowers in these pictures
look like the names
that people have given them?

Lady's-slipper

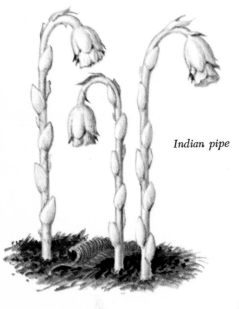

Indian pipe

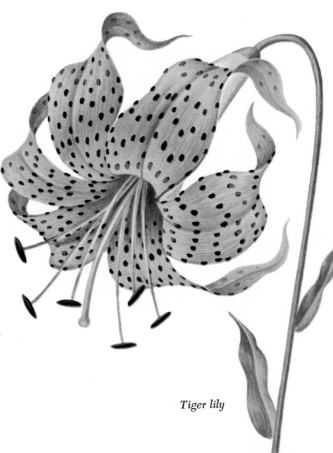

Buttercup

Tiger lily

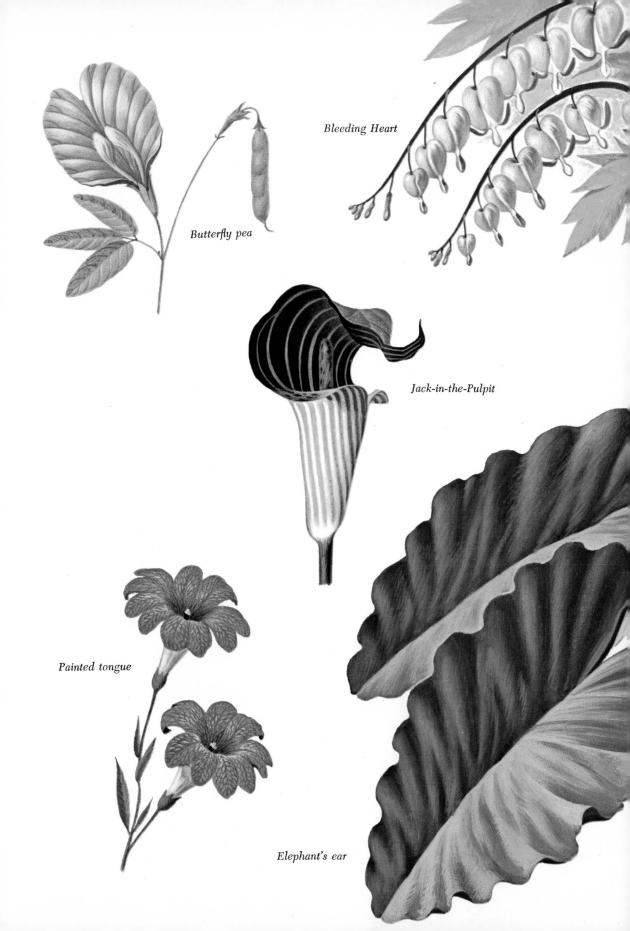

Butterfly pea

Bleeding Heart

Jack-in-the-Pulpit

Painted tongue

Elephant's ear

Things That Happen to Me

I get blisters when my shoe rubs,
but how do I get them?
I get black-and-blue marks
when I fall down,
but why do I get them?
I sweat when I'm hot,
but where does sweat come from?
I cry when I'm hurt,
but where do tears come from?
I get freckles on my nose,
but where do they come from?
Do goose bumps come from geese?
Or warts from toads?

To find the answers to these questions,
read the next few pages.

WHERE DO TEARS COME FROM?

Tears keep coming all the time—even when I don't cry. The tears come from tiny sacs, called glands, that are in the corner of my eye.

Muscles in my eyelids tighten and squeeze tears out of the tear glands everytime I blink my eyes. The tears wash my eyes and help to keep them clean and healthy.

But when I cry, my eyes get a shower bath—a bath of tears. Sometimes they spill out of my eyes and run down my cheeks. Sometimes they run down tiny openings in the corner of my eyes and into my nose.

WHERE DO WARTS COME FROM?

Toads, rabbits, and cattle can get warts. And so can I. But I can't get a wart from any of these animals. I can get a wart only from a virus—a tiny living thing too small to see unless you use a special microscope.

A wart is a growth caused by a virus on the top layer of

WANT TO HOLD MY TOAD?

the skin. It usually does not hurt or do any harm. Sometimes it goes away by itself. But if a wart hurts, a doctor has to remove it.

Warts can grow anywhere on the skin, and can be different sizes and shapes. Flat warts sometimes grow on the feet. Warts that look like little beards sometimes grow on the face. Warts that look like little cauliflowers sometimes grow on the hands.

WHERE DO FRECKLES COME FROM?

Where did I get those tiny spots
dotting my arms
and sprinkled across the bridge of my nose?
They are not dirt spots
or chocolate spots.
They are freckles!

Freckles pop out on my skin
after I have been out in the sun.
Almost everyone has special chemicals
called pigments in their skin.
And one kind of pigment, called melanin,
gives the brown color to the skin.

The sun makes the melanin come out in my skin.
And that is why I get a suntan.
Freckles are just tiny spots in my skin
that have more melanin in them
than the rest of my skin.
And so they pop out as dark spots.

Freckle King

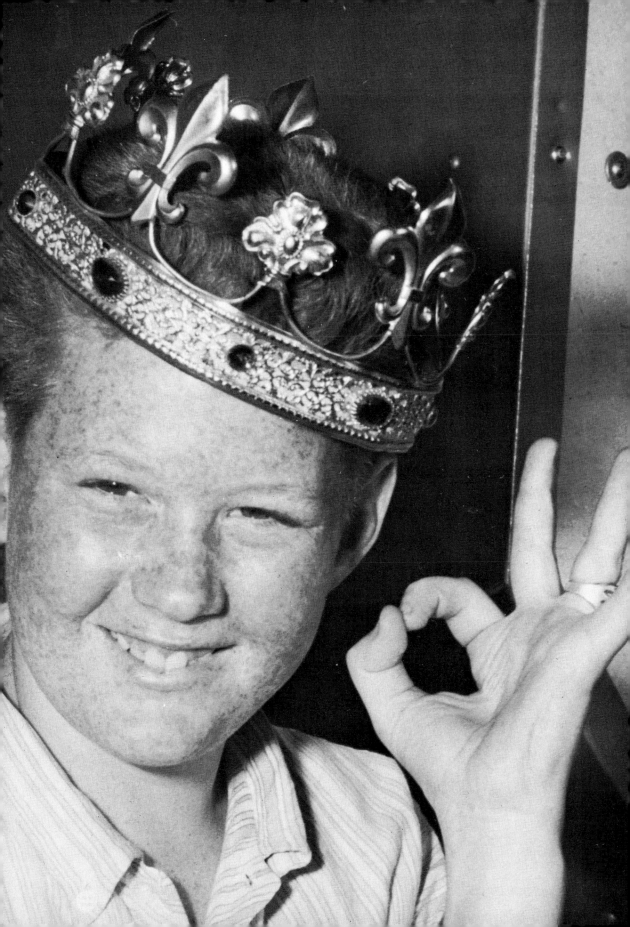

WHERE DOES SWEAT COME FROM?

It's hot and I'm sweating.
Where does the sweat come from?

When I get too warm,
tiny tubes called sweat glands,
that are just under my skin,
push sweat through tiny holes, called pores,
in my skin.

Sweat is mostly water mixed with salt.
I can taste the salt
when I lick a drop of sweat
with my tongue.

If I sweat a lot, I get thirsty
and feel droopy.
Then I have to drink water
and take salt pills
to replace the sweat and the salt
that was pushed out of my pores.

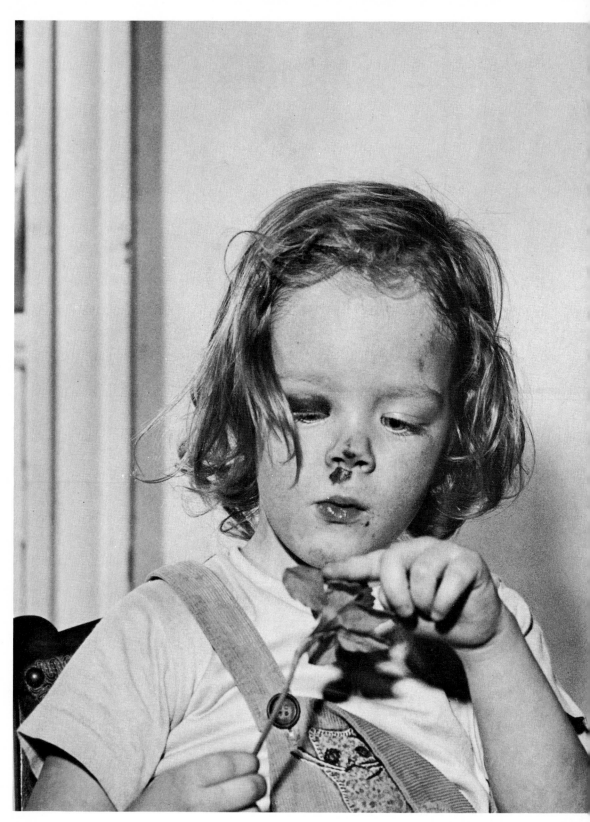

WHERE DO BLACK-AND-BLUE MARKS COME FROM?

When I fall down, I sometimes get a scratch on my knee, or a skinned knee, or just a red bump on my knee.

The bump is red for a little while, but then it starts to turn black and blue. This happens because I broke some tiny blood vessels under the skin when I fell. And blood from the broken blood vessels oozes around the red bump. The blood that gets trapped makes the bump black and blue.

In a few days the black and blue bump turns green and yellow because the blood starts to ooze away from the bump.

Soon the bump disappears!

HOW DO I GET GOOSE BUMPS?

I'm cold and I've got goose bumps!
And where there's a bump,
there's a hair.
And where there's a hair,
there's a tiny muscle in my skin.

When I get cold, or angry or frightened,
the tiny muscles in my skin
shrink or tighten up.
They make my hair stand on end.
And that's why I get goose bumps.

WHY
DO I
GET BLISTERS?

A blister is a bump of watery stuff,
called tissue fluid,
that pops up when I get a burn—
a burn when my shoe rubs my foot,
or when I touch a hot stove,
or when I get a bad sunburn.

Tiny tubes in my body
make and squeeze the watery stuff
over the burn.
The watery stuff protects the burned skin
and stops the burn
from hurting too much.

Sometimes when my finger gets caught
in a door, I get a red blister
because I broke a tiny blood vessel
under the skin.
The blood oozes out,
and I get a blood blister
instead of a water blister.

WHAT'S A FEVER?

I always have a temperature,
but I don't always have a fever.
I can take my temperature
by putting a thermometer
under my tongue or under my armpit
for about five minutes.
When I'm feeling well,
the thermometer shows
that my temperature is about 98.6° F.

But when I have a fever,
my temperature shoots up—
sometimes as high as 103° or more.

A fever means
that I have an infection or a disease.

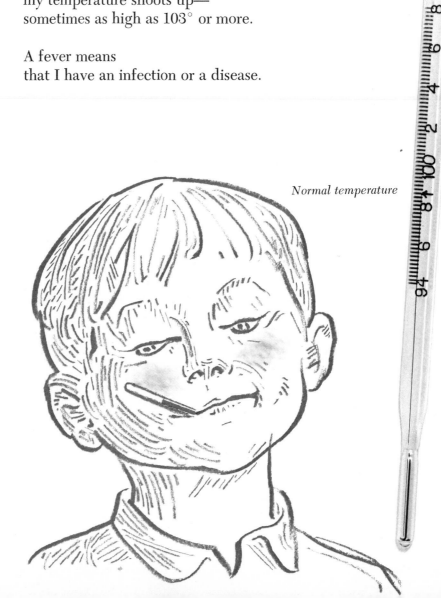

Normal temperature

Doctors don't know exactly how
a disease causes fever.
Maybe it's because
the germs of an infection
won't let my body give off heat
as fast as it does
when I don't have a fever.
Whatever the reason,
when I have a fever,
I need the rest and medicine
that a doctor says I should take
to help make me well.

When the medicine works on me,
down goes my temperature
to about 98.6°.
I still have a temperature,
but I don't have a fever.

*Above normal
temperature*

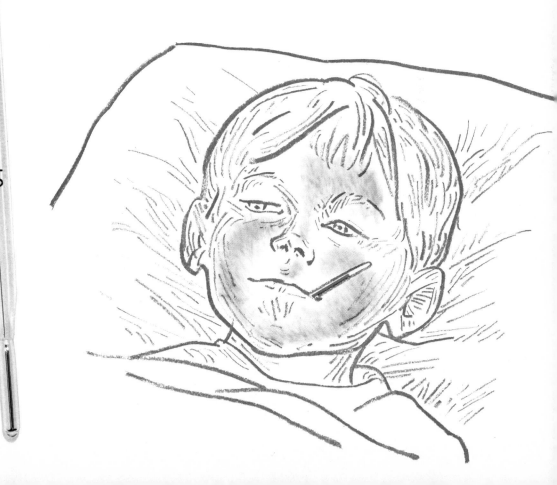

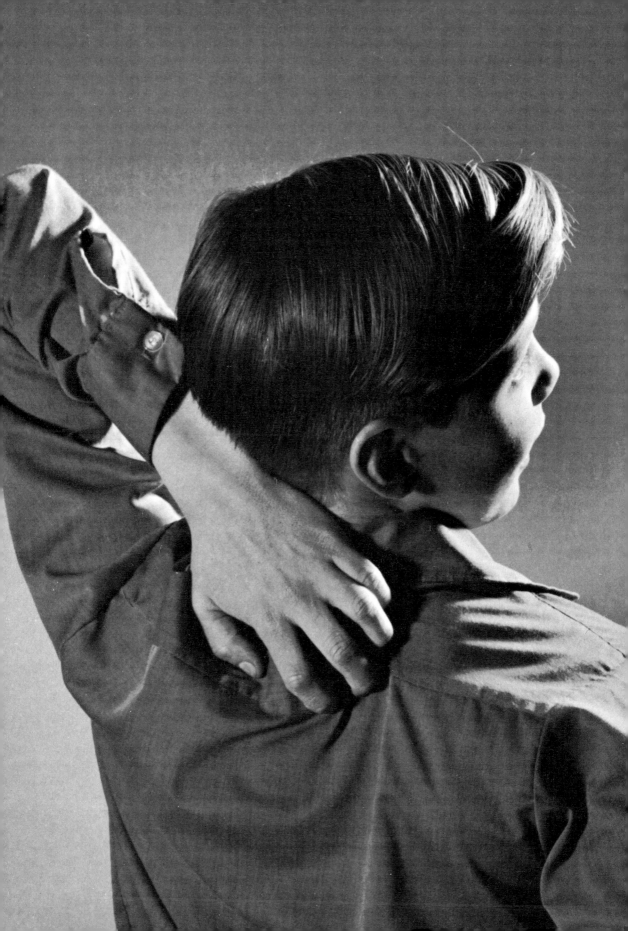

WHAT'S AN ITCH?

I have an itch.
Is it a nibbling flea that I can't see,
or is it something in the soap I washed with
that makes me itch?
Whatever it is,
my brain is getting the message
through tiny nerves
that are just under the top layer of my skin.

The outside of my skin connects
with many different kinds of nerves.
These nerves connect with my brain.
Some nerves carry messages about touch to my brain.
Some carry messages about heat and cold.
Some carry messages about pain.
Sometimes the nerves that carry messages about pain
also carry messages about itches.

Hurting pain never makes me want to scratch.
It throbs or stabs too much.
But I always want to scratch an itch
because it tickles and prickles.

I know that I shouldn't scratch an itch—
I might break the skin and let germs in.
But when I get an itch,
I itch to scratch the itch—
don't you?

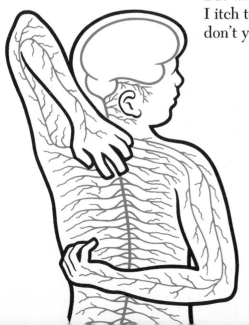

WHY DO I GET CHAPPED SKIN?

My skin is red and rough and cracked.
That means my skin is chapped.
How does chapping happen?

I have tiny tubes called oil glands
just under the top layer of my skin.
The oil flows through the tubes
to almost invisible holes,
called pores, in my skin.
The oil protects my skin
from becoming too dry.
But in cold weather,
the air can dry up so much of the natural oil
on my skin that my skin can get chapped.
If I lick my lips too much,
I lick away the natural oil that protects them,
and my lips get dry and chapped.
And if I wash my hands and face with strong soap,
the soap and water may wash away even more
of the natural oil on my skin.
Then it's even harder for me
to keep from getting chapped skin.

If my skin gets chapped,
I can put cold cream or petroleum jelly on it
because I know that these things
take the place of the oil that my skin has lost.
Then my chapped skin heals.

How Animals Act

Is there a bird that dances upside down
or a fly that dances a jig?

Is there an animal that stands on its head
or one that dances when it finds food?

Is there an animal that makes noises with its wings
or a fish that makes noises with its teeth?

Is there a bird that paints a playhouse
or a spider that brings presents?

Is there a fish that has a place all its own
or an animal that plays hide-and-seek?

Is there a bird that says its name?
Or a bird that speaks words?
Or an animal which lives in the sea
that can even imitate
words that people use?

Read on and see.

ANIMAL DANCES

When we move our feet to music, we are dancing. But did you know that some birds do a high-flying dance, an upside-down dance, or a strutting dance?

The bluebird of paradise hangs upside down from a tree branch when it dances! First, it sits on the branch and calls until another bluebird comes to watch. Then, holding tight to the branch, it lowers itself backward until it is hanging upside down. Then it starts its dance. It shakes and fans out its beautiful blue plumes, and rocks its body to and fro so that the plumes flutter.

The high-flying woodcock starts its dance on the ground. It struts and twitters and pushes out its chest. Then it whirls and flies high into the sky. It tailspins down—almost making a crash landing, but it stops just in time and lands on its feet.

UP-AND-DOWN JIG

The May fly is not a bird, but it does a dance, too—an up-and-down jig in the air. It flies up in a straight line—stops—and drops down again, using its wings like a parachute.

SWAYING HEADS

A snake, called an adder, dances with another adder. The snakes raise the front part of their bodies straight up and sway their heads from side to side.

317

Showing Off

Some people show off to try and get the attention of others.
But did you know that some animals are show-offs, too?

The peacock fans out its beautiful feathers
and struts back and forth
"proud as a peacock" for all to see.

When the whale shows off,
it lashes the water with its tail,
rolls over on its back, and even stands on its head.
Then it leaps out of the water high into the air.

The water rat shows off
by turning around in the water so fast
that it makes a whirlpool.

The otter tumbles and splashes
in and out of the water,
wiggling and waggling its tail.

The stone marten lifts its head,
curves its tail, stiffens its legs,
and raises the hair on its back when it shows off.

MALLARDS HAVE MANNERS

When a boy mallard duck and a girl mallard duck meet,
first they take a drink of water.
Then the boy mallard slides his bill against his wing
to make a sound like a tiny wooden rattle.
The girl mallard watches and then does the same thing.

Next, the boy mallard shakes his head
forward and upward,
forward and upward,
over and over,
again and again.

Then it thrusts its bill in and out of the water
and whistles and grunts.
The two mallard ducks have met.
Now they are friends.

Animal Noisemakers

You can make noises
by clapping your hands,
stamping your feet,
beating a drum,
banging a pot, or clanging a bell.

But some animals make noises
by hitting and rubbing parts of their bodies.

Crickets, katydids, and grasshoppers
rub their wings together to make a noise.

A bird called a sharp-tailed grouse
makes a noise with its wings when it dances.

And the hummingbird
beats its wings so fast that they whir and hum.

An insect called a locust
rubs its back legs against its wings to make loud noises.
It also beats its wings together to make clacking noises.

One kind of fish, called a drumfish,
makes a booming echo with its teeth.

A bird called a woodpecker
drums on a tree with its bill.

grasshopper

drumfish

sharp-tailed grouse   *woodpecker*

Chirps, Coos, and Cries

You don't have to see a bird
to tell what kind it is.
Just listen to its call.

Some birds seem to say their name
like
Chick-a-dee-dee-dee-dee,
Fee-bee,
Bob-o-lee, bob-o-link,
Whip-poor-will,
Kill-deer, kill-deer.

Some birds seem to say words
like
the ROBIN that calls
    Cheer-up cheerily,
and the EASTERN TOWHEE that says
    Drink your tea-e-e.
The WHITE-THROATED SPARROW calls
    Peabody, Peabody, Peabody.
The GREAT HORNED OWL says
    Who who-who who who who,
and the OVENBIRD calls
    Teacher! Teacher! Teacher!

But some birds just make funny noises
like
the RED-WINGED BLACKBIRD that says
    Konk-ka-ree,
the CARDINAL that calls
    Whoit, whoit, whoit, whit, whit, whit,
the MOURNING DOVE that says
    Coo-coo-coo,
the ROOSTER that crows
    Cock-a-doodle-doo,
the CROCODILE BIRD that calls
    Zic-zac,
the RAVEN that says
    Cr-r-ruck,
the LAUGHING GULL that says
    Ha, ha, ha,
and the CROW that calls
    Caw, caw, caw.

A BIRD THAT PAINTS
ITS HOUSE

Imagine a bird that builds a playhouse, and then paints it and decorates it with flowers and knickknacks. That's what a bowerbird does!

The playhouse is a little room with twigs propped up on each side. The bowerbird paints the inside of the playhouse with a paint it makes of chewed-up bark or charcoal. What does it use as a paintbrush? Its beak!

It decorates the playhouse with bright objects like feathers, shells, silverware, broken glass, and nails. It also puts fresh flowers at the entrance every day.

ANIMAL PRESENTS

Some boy animals bring presents to their girl animal friends. Some boy penguins give pebbles to their girl friends. Boy jackdaws, ravens, and crows bring sticks to their girl friends. Boy flies called dance flies bring their girl friends balloons of silk. Boy wolf spiders and foxes bring food to their girl friends.

Private—Keep Out!

People have fences to keep other people out, and they even put up signs that read, "Keep Out." Some animals also have places they keep other animals out of. They cannot put up fences or signs, but they fight off animals that try to come into what they think is their special place.

A fish called a firemouth has a special place that it chases other fish away from. The place is usually between two rocks. When another fish comes near, the firemouth chases it and tries to bite it. If the fish doesn't move, the firemouth stiffens its fins, circles around the fish, and tries to beat it with its tail or butt it with its head. The fish usually gives up and swims off.

A seal's special place is a part of the beach. Boy seals protect these places from other boy seals. They bellow and sway and bite and slash one another. The boy seal that wins its fights and keeps its special place is called a beachmaster.

Some frogs and birds have special places that they protect, too.

Coheleach

FIREFLY BEACON

On a hot summer night
you may suddenly see
bright, little flashes of light—
a firefly beacon—
blinking on and off,
on and off.

Fireflies signal to each other with flashes of light.
The on-and-off flashes help a boy firefly find a girl firefly.
The boy firefly lights his beacon.
The girl firefly sees it.
And exactly two seconds later, she flashes her light.
The boy firefly sees the light and flies toward it.
The fireflies flash their lights
on and off,
on and off,
until they meet.

MEETING IN THE AIR

Some boy ants and girl ants have wings, and meet in the air.
They fly high into the sky
and then drop to earth one by one.
The boy ants die,
but the girl ants rip off their own wings,
look for a new home,
and start to lay eggs for a new ant colony.

ANIMAL STRUMMERS AND SHOOTERS

Sometimes when a boy wants to see a girl,
he stands under her window singing and strumming a guitar.
When a boy spider wants to call a girl spider,
he plunks on the thread of the spider web until she comes out.

Have you ever sent a valentine with a picture
of Dan Cupid shooting an arrow?
Sometimes a snail acts like Cupid.
But a snail shoots a hard piece of shell at another snail.

331

Hide-and-Seek

When you play hide-and-seek, you probably close your eyes, count to ten, and call out, "Here I come, ready or not!" before you start looking.

Some animals play hide-and-seek, too.

A girl water shrew hides in mole holes or under stones and waits for a boy water shrew to find her. Or the girl water shrew may dive from the bank into a lake, run underwater across the bottom, and find a hiding place on the bank at the other side of the lake.

Deer play hide-and-seek by running from each other. The girl deer calls to the boy deer, and then she starts running. The boy deer chases her. The girl deer runs around and around in circles and then dashes off into high bushes where the boy deer has a hard time finding her.

Cuckoo birds play hide-and-seek in treetops. The birds fly, flit, and dash from tree to tree chasing each other.

Why Honeybees Dance

People and many animals dance for fun. But a honeybee dances to tell other honeybees where to find nectar.

Honeybees get their food from the nectar and the pollen of flowers. When a honeybee scout finds flowers, it gathers some of the nectar and flies back to the hive.

If the flowers are close to the hive, the bee scout dances a round dance to show the other bees where the flowers are. It dances around one way, turns, and dances around the other way. Soon the other bees join the dance. The bee scout lets the other bees taste the nectar. Then the bees leave the hive to find the flowers.

If the flowers are far from the hive, the bee scout does a wigwag
dance to show the others where the flowers are. The bee scout
dances straight forward in a line, circles one way, and goes back
to the starting point. Then it dances straight forward again and
circles the other way, over and over, again and again, as it wig-
wags its body.

The straight line tells the other bees in what direction the
flowers are, and the speed of the wigwagging tells them how far
away the flowers are.

When honeybees gather nectar and pollen from flowers, they
also carry pollen from one flower to another. Then the flowers
can make new seeds, and the new seeds will grow into new
flowers.

DO DOLPHINS TALK?

Children in France speak French.
Children in Spain speak Spanish.
Children in China speak Chinese.
And dolphins speak dolphinese.

A dolphin is an animal that lives in the water.
It can talk to other dolphins,
but we do not always understand what it is saying.

Dolphins say different things at different times.
When a dolphin is alone, it whistles and clicks.
When one dolphin talks to another,
it whistles, clicks, and quacks.
And when many dolphins play together,
they whistle, click, quack, squawk, and blat.

A dolphin in trouble sends out a signal for help.
It is an up-and-down squeal.
All the other dolphins that hear the sound come and help.

Dolphins can imitate the sounds that people make, too.
They can laugh the way we laugh
and whistle the way we whistle,
and some say they can even imitate some of our words.

Maybe someday, if we find out
what the whistles, clicks, quacks,
squawks, and blats mean,
and if dolphins can learn what our words mean,
we will be able to talk to dolphins
and they will be able to talk to us.

About Me and Others

Most animals can see.
And so can I.

Most animals can hear.
And so can I.

Most animals can feel.
And so can I.

Most animals grow.
And so do I.

Most animals sleep.
And so do I.

Most animals have mothers and fathers.
And so do I.

Why am I different?

When I see, I can know what I see.
When I hear, I can know what I hear.
When I feel, I can know what I feel.
And if I don't know, I can find out!

When I grow, I grow only so big and no bigger.
When I sleep, I sleep in a bed.
And when my mother and father come into a room,
I know who they are.

I am ME.
And there is no one else in the world just like ME.

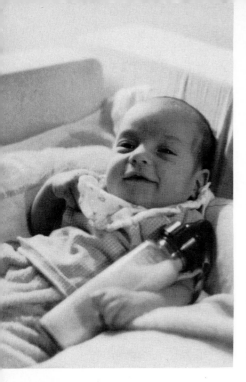

FIRST I WAS A BABY

Once there wasn't any me.
Then from my mother I was born.
I was a helpless little baby
who slept, ate, and cried.
I could not talk or walk.
And I could not feed or dress myself.
My mother and my father did everything for me.

But babies grow fast.
And soon I was able to sit up and see
the things around me.
Next I started to crawl,
then I stood,
and then I walked and talked.

I am still growing, and each day I can do a little more
than I could do the day before.
It takes a long time for boys and girls to grow up.
But I know I will be grownup someday.

GROWING

Children grow like people,
Kittens grow like cats;
Puppies grow like doggies,
And mice, they grow like rats.

Grass grows like a flower,
And a bush grows like a tree;
But my clothes don't seem
   to grow at all,
So they're too small for me.

PATRICIA ALICE FISHER
(*written at age 9*)

I Can Learn

Some animals learn from their parents.
And so do I.
But I can learn more than any animal can.

I can ask questions
and read or be read to.
I can watch others and learn from them.
I can learn from people that lived long ago.
And I can learn from people in other lands
because I can learn to read the books they wrote
and learn to understand what they say
on radio and television.

And I can think about
what I ask,
or read,
or hear,
or watch.

EYES
ARE FOR
SEEING

When I see a flower,
it might look like this.

When a dog sees
the same flower,
it might look like this.

And when a bee sees
the same flower,
it might look like this.

Most animals see with two eyes, just as I do. But their eyes
are different from mine.

A rabbit has two eyes, but they are on the sides of its head.
It can see an enemy sneaking up from behind without turning
its head.

A hippopotamus has two eyes, but they are on top of its head.
It can stay underwater yet keep its eyes above the water
watching for danger.

A lion can see well in the dark and can hunt for food at night.

A bee has two big eyes. But each big eye is made of many,
many tiny eyes. So a bee sees many flowers when it looks at
only one.

I can see all the colors of the rainbow, so can monkeys and
apes. Bees, moths, and fireflies can see still another color, called
ultraviolet. But most animals see only gray, black, and white.

Sound-Catchers

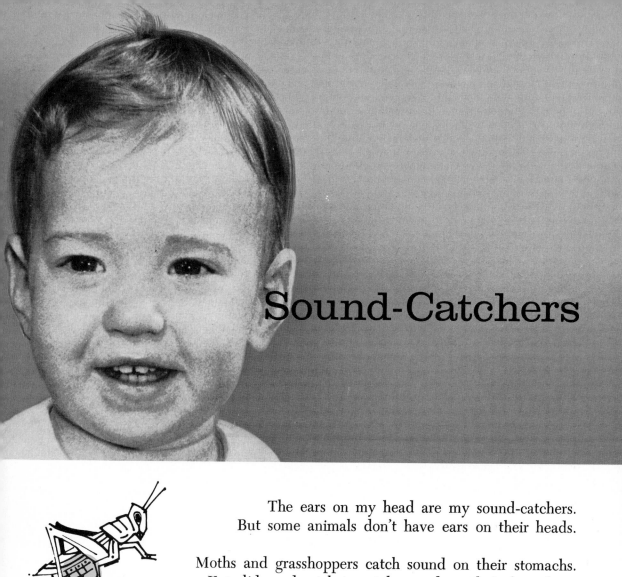

The ears on my head are my sound-catchers.
But some animals don't have ears on their heads.

Moths and grasshoppers catch sound on their stomachs.
Katydids and crickets catch sound on their front legs.
Cockroaches catch sound on their tails.
Water beetles catch sound on their chests.
And blowflies catch sound on their wings.

346

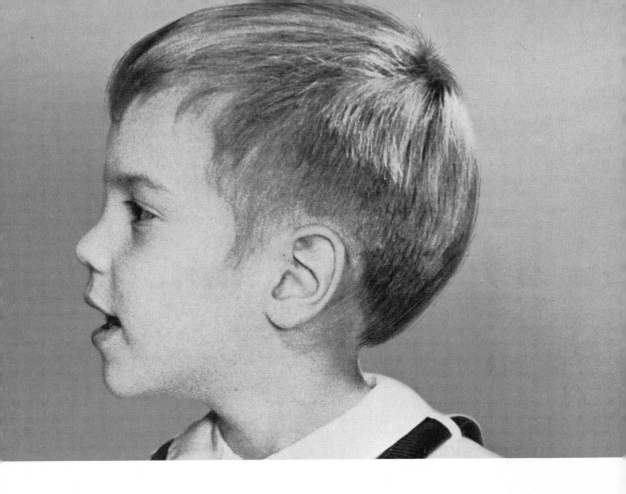

I can hear low sounds, high sounds, and in-between sounds.
But some animals can hear sounds that I can't hear.

A chimpanzee can hear higher sounds than I can.
And a dog can hear higher sounds than a chimpanzee can.
A rat can hear higher sounds than a dog can.
And a cat can hear higher sounds than a rat can.
A bat can hear the highest sounds of all.

OUCH!

If I stick a pin in my finger or pinch myself—
Ouch! It hurts.

If I put my hand on a hot stove—
Yipe! It burns.

If I touch a piece of ice—
Br-r-r-r! It's cold.

If I rub a feather on my foot—
Ha! Ha! It tickles.

I can feel pain, heat, cold, and tickles all over my body.
And if someone pats me on my back,
I know he is there even though I don't see him.

Inside my body are many threadlike wires called nerves.
Some of my nerves are big, but most of them are tiny.
All my nerves, both big and small, are connected to my brain.
When I stick a pin into my finger,
the nerves in my finger send a warning message to my brain.
And my brain tells me that my finger hurts.
The message travels so fast that I know my finger hurts
as soon as I stick the pin into it.

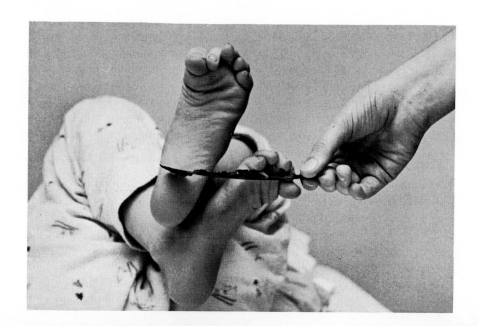

349

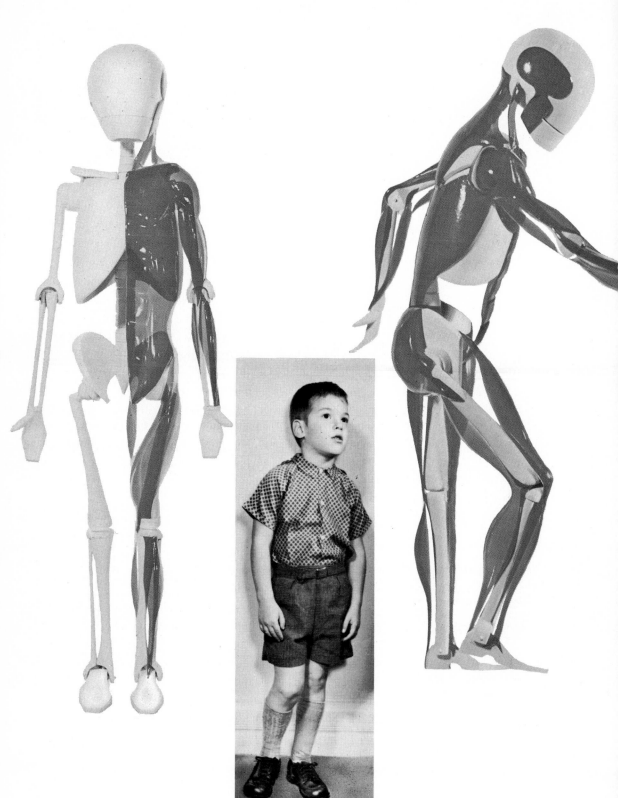

WHAT
HOLDS ME TOGETHER?

Boards hold houses together. Steel beams hold big skyscrapers together. And the bones in my body hold me together. Without my bones, I would be as soft and as floppy as a rag doll.

My bones are straight and hard and do not bend. But I can bend my fingers and toes, my ankles and knees, my shoulders, wrists, and elbows because my bones meet at these places. Where they meet, I have joints. And I can bend, twist, or turn my body at the joint places.

Muscles are connected to the bones and to the joints in my body. They move the bones when I want to move.

My bones, joints, and muscles work together so that I can get up, lie down, sit up, stand up, run, jump, and walk.

THE PUMPS INSIDE ME

When I put my hand on my chest, I can
feel my heart thumping. It's thumping
because it's pumping. My heart pumps
blood through thousands of tiny pipes
that are inside my body, all the way from
the tips of my toes to the top of my head.
My blood moves through the pipes and
carries food, air, and water.

When I put my hand on my chest,
I can feel another kind of pump, too.
This pump is an air pump.
My chest moves slowly out and slowly in,
over and over again.
A muscle, called the diaphragm, moves it.
When my chest moves out,
fresh air is pulled inside me.
When my chest moves in,
used air is pushed outside me.

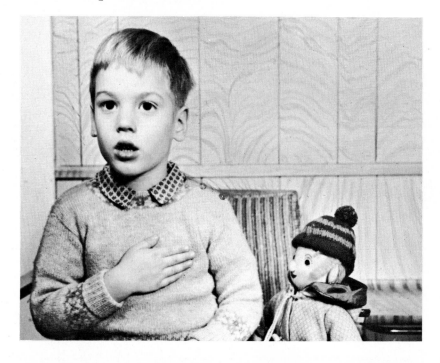

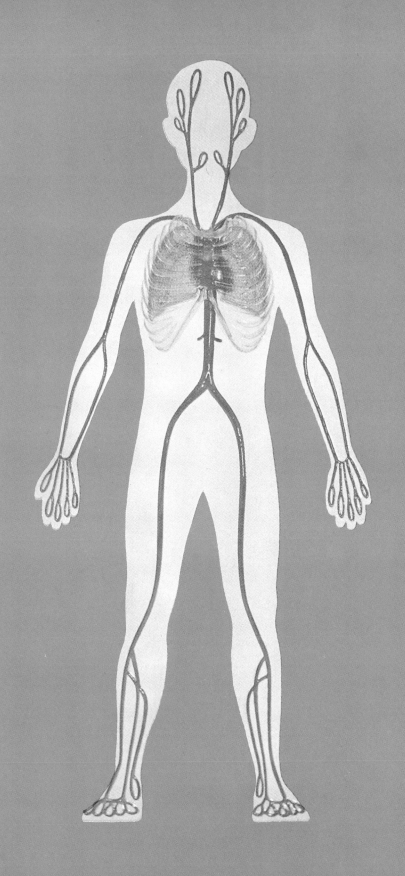

I SMELL,
I TASTE,
I CHEW,
I EAT

Hm-m-m-m-m! My mother made some cookies.
I know they are chocolate cookies
because they smell like chocolate cookies.
In my nose are tiny nerves that send messages to my brain.
And my brain tells me that I smell chocolate cookies.

I know they are chocolate cookies
because they taste like chocolate cookies.
On my tongue there are tiny nerves, called taste buds,
that send messages to my brain.

And my brain tells me
that I taste chocolate cookies.

When I bite into a cooky,
I use my front teeth,
which are biters.
But I mash the cooky
with my back teeth,
which are chewers.

After I chew the cooky, I swallow it.
And it goes down my throat
through a long tube
into my stomach.

The cooky is mashed
even more in my stomach.
The mashed-up cooky—
and all the food I eat—
gives my body energy
so that I can run, jump,
play, and grow.

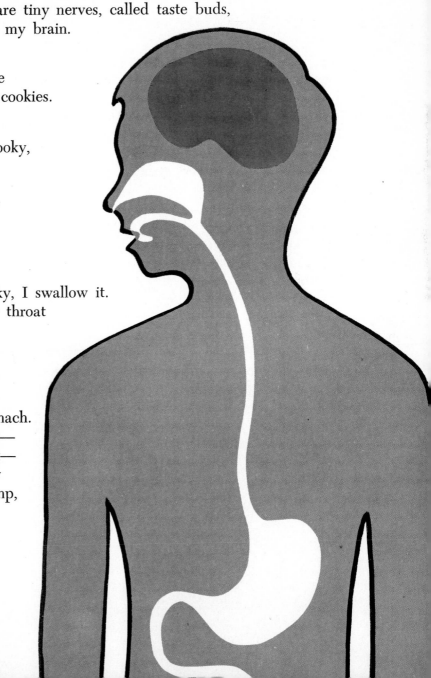

How I Grow

As I grow taller,
my legs and arms,
hands and feet,
head, heart, lungs, brain,
stomach, teeth, nose,
mouth, muscles, bones,
and all the other parts of my body get bigger.

I may not think they do because I cannot see them growing.
When I get up in the morning,
my body doesn't seem any bigger
than it was the night before.
But my body is growing all the time.
It keeps growing until I am as big as I am going to be.
And then I am grown up.

Some plants and animals grow up fast.
A horse grows fast,
and so does a mouse, dog, cat,
tulip, dandelion, jonquil, or violet.
But some plants and animals
seem to take forever to grow.

357

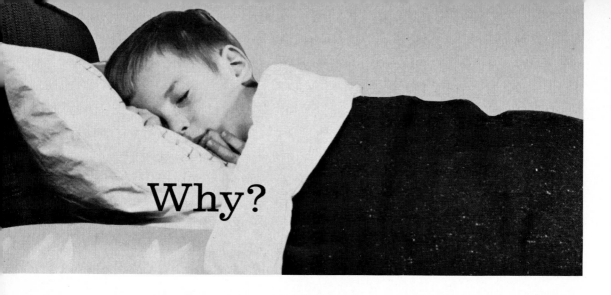

Why?

WHY DO I SLEEP?

I sleep because my body needs rest and so does my brain, which must have sleep more than any other part of my body. If I did not get enough sleep, I would be too tired to think—too tired to act the way I should.

WHY DO I SNEEZE?

I sneeze when something gets into my nose that doesn't belong there. As I breathe, little hairs in my nose catch dirt and dust from the air. But sometimes a piece of dust gets past the hairs. That piece of dust does not belong in my nose. So the nerves inside my nose make me sneeze. And I keep sneezing until the sneeze blows the piece of dust out.

WHY DO I SHIVER?

My body is warm. When I am too warm, my body sweats through tiny openings in my skin. But when I get cold, the tiny openings close up. If I get too cold, I shiver. My muscles move all by themselves to warm me up. That's what shivering is.

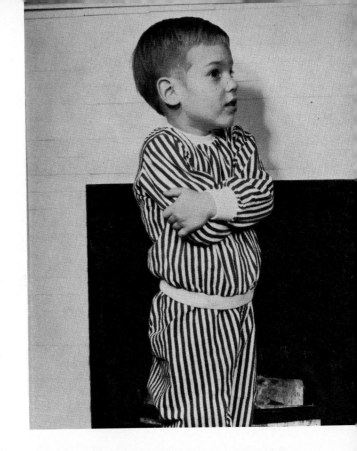

WHY DO I HICCUP?

When I breathe, a muscle, called the diaphragm, pulls air into my lungs and pushes it out. If for some reason my diaphragm jerks suddenly, air rushes past my voice box, and out comes a HIC instead of a breath.

WHY DO I YAWN?

I yawn when I am tired. But I also yawn when my body isn't getting enough fresh air. When I yawn, I breathe in big gulps of fresh air and breathe out big gulps of stale air.

I Speak,
I Say,
I Talk

Cats purr.
Lions roar.
Owls hoot.
Bears snore.
Crickets creak.
Mice squeak.
Sheep baa.
But I SPEAK!

Monkeys chatter.
Cows moo.
Ducks quack.
Doves coo.
Pigs squeal.
Horses neigh.
Chickens cluck.
But I SAY!

Flies hum.
Dogs growl.
Bats screech.
Coyotes howl.
Frogs croak.
Parrots squawk.
Bees buzz.
But I TALK!

ARNOLD L. SHAPIRO

Illustration
Acknowledgments

The publishers of CHILDCRAFT gratefully acknowledge the courtesy of the following artists, photographers, publishers, agencies, and corporations for illustrations in the volume. Page numbers refer to two-page spreads. The words "(*left*)," "(*center*)," "(*top*)," "(*bottom*)," and "(*right*)," indicate position on the spread. All illustrations are the exclusive property of the publishers of CHILDCRAFT unless names are marked with an asterisk (*).

LIVING THINGS:

4–5: Francis Chase
6–7: Vernon McKissack
8–9: Raymond Perlman
10–11: Vernon McKissack

COMING INTO THE WORLD:

12–13: Francis Chase
14–15: art by Everett McNear; photos (*top to bottom*) Carleton Ray, New York Zoological Society (*), Alfa Studio, W. Suschitzky (*), W. Suschitzky (*)
16–17: (*left*) W. Suschitzky (*); (*top right*) Ylla, Rapho-Guillumette (*), (*bottom right*) Ray Atkeson (*)
18–19: art by Paul McNear; photo, Ford Motor Company (*)
20–21: photo, Eastern Photo Service (*); art by Raymond Perlman
22–23: art by Francis Chase; photos by Bruce Roberts, P.I.P. (*)
24–25: Francis Chase
26–27: (*top left*) courtesy Fleischmann Laboratories, Standard Brands, Inc., (*) (*bottom left*) Willis Peterson (*), Paul L. Miller (*); (*right*) Willis Peterson (*)
28–29: (*top*) Hans Cordes (*), (*bottom left*) Cy La Tour, (*bottom right*) Otto Croy (*)
30–31: (*left*) Gene Wolfsheimer (*); (*right*) Miami Seaquarium (*)
32–33: art by Everett McNear; photo, *Tropical Fish Hobbyist* Magazine (*)
34–35: William Vandivert (*)
36–37: Stan Galli
38–39: Charles Harper

GROWING UP:

40–41: Francis Chase
42–43: (*left*) Oscar Greenleaf (*); (*right*) Jack Dermid, National Audubon Society (*)
44–45: art by René Martin; photo by John H. Gerard (*)
46–47: art by Vernon McKissack; photo by John H. Gerard (*)
48–49: Eliot Porter (*)
50–51: John Solie—Stevens-Gross Studios, Inc.
52–53: art by Everett McNear; photo by David Fleay (*)
54–55: George Lopac—Stephens Biondi De Cicco Inc.
56–57: Richard Keane
58–59: photos, (*left*) Walter Chandoha (*), (*right*) Ylla, Rapho-Guillumette (*); art by Charles Harper
60–61: Fred Mayer, Black Star (*)
62–63: Stan Galli
64–65: Guy J. Coheleach

FINDING THINGS TO EAT:

66–67: Bob Kuhn
68–69: art by Charles Harper; photo by Walter Chandoha (*)
70–71: Rudolph Zallinger
72–73: Rudolph and Jean Zallinger
74–75: (*left*) Walter Chandoha (*); (*right*) Birnback (*)

76–77: art by René Martin; photo by Cy La Tour
78–79: photo by Eliot Porter (*); art by Rudolf Freund
80–81: New York Zoological Society (*)
82–83: Ylla, Rapho-Guillumette (*)
84–85: Bob Kuhn
86–87: (*left*) G. Ronald Austin, National Audubon Society (*); (*right*) Otto Meyer, National Audubon Society (*)
88–89: (*left*) Roy Pinney, Photo-Library, Inc. (*); (*right*) Chicago Natural History Museum (*)
90–91: Raymond Perlman
92–93: Rudolf Freund
94–95: Eraldo Carugati—Stephens Biondi De Cicco Inc.
96–97: photo, Eastern Photo Service (*); art by Raymond Perlman
98–99: Paul McNear
100–101: Raymond Perlman

WHERE THEIR HOMES ARE:

102–103: Raymond Perlman
104–105: Andreas Feininger, courtesy *Life* Magazine © 1953 Time Inc. (*)
106–107: (*left*) J. W. Jackson (*); (*right*) G. M. Bradt (*)
108–109: art by Bob Kuhn; photo by William Vandivert (*)
110–111: Raymond Perlman
112–113: (*left*) Ethel Spencer, Photo-Library, Inc. (*), Bird Photographs Inc. (*), Allan D. Cruickshank, National Audubon Society (*); (*right*) John H. Gerard, National Audubon Society (*), Allan D. Cruickshank, National Audubon Society (*)
114–115: George Suyeoka
116–117: (*left*) Grant Heilman (*); (*right*) Verna R. Johnson, National Audubon Society (*)
118–119: art by Everett McNear; photo by Garth Grant-Thomson, Annan Photo Feature (*)
120–121: (*left*) James H. Brown; (*right*) Ross E. Hutchins (*)
122–123: (*left*) CHILDCRAFT photo; (*right*) Lynwood M. Chace (*)
124–125: art by Rudolf Freund; photo by G. M. Bradt (*)
126–127: Charles Harper
128–129: Bob Kuhn

MOVING AROUND:

130–131: Francis Chase
132–133: Paul McNear
134–135: photo, New York Zoological Society (*); art by Guy J. Coheleach
136–137: art by Vernon McKissack; photo by Charles E. Lane (*)
138–139: Charles Harper
140–141: (*left*) Ben Schneider (*); (*right*) Don Stebbing
142–143: photo by John H. Gerard, National Audubon Society (*); art by Paul McNear
144–145: art by Guy J. Coheleach; photo by Charles T. Berry (*)
146–147: art by Charles Harper; photo by Robert C. Hermes, National Audubon Society (*)
148–149: (*left*) Leonard Lee Rue III, National Audubon Society (*); (*right*) H. E. Edgerton, National Audubon Society (*)
150–151: Vernon McKissack
152–153: (*left*) George Porter, National Audubon Society (*); (*right*) Cy La Tour (*)
154–155: Francis Chase

WHEN TO CHANGE HOMES:

156–157: Bob Kuhn
158–159: Grant Heilman (*)
160–161: Vernon McKissack
162–163: (*left*) Karl W. Kenyon, National Audubon Society (*); (*right*) John Dominis, *Life* Magazine © Time Inc. (*)
164–165: Everett McNear
166–167: photo by Frank Lane (*)
168–169: art by Everett McNear; photo by Cy La Tour
170–171: photo by Hugh M. Halliday (*); art by Paul McNear
172–173: Bob Kuhn
174–175: (*left*) John H. Gerard (*); (*right*) Mitchell Campbell (*)

GUARDING THEIR LIVES:

176–177: Francis Chase
178–179: (*left*) New York Zoological Society (°); (*right*) David Linton (°)
180–181: Guy J. Coheleach
182–183: photo by Jan Player (°); art by Everett McNear
184–185: (*left*) New York Zoological Society (°); (*right*) Franklin Williamson, Black Star (°)
186–187: (*left*) Cal Roy—Swan Studios, Inc.; (*top right*) Professor Grzimek, Frankfurt (°); (*bottom right*) Dade Thornton, National Audubon Society (°)
188–189: photo by Ylla, Rapho-Guillumette (°); art by Guy J. Coheleach
190–191: art by Paul McNear; photo by Willis Peterson (°)
192–193: (*left*) New York Zoological Society (°), Photo-Library, Inc. (°); (*right*) John H. Gerard (°)
194–195: Bob Kuhn
196–197: (*left*) Leonard Lee Rue III, National Audubon Society (°); (*right*) Cy La Tour (°)
198–199: art by Charles Harper; photo by Lynwood M. Chace, National Audubon Society (°)
200–201: art by Everett McNear; photos by (*top*) James Simon, Photo Researchers (°), (*bottom*) Des Bartlett (°)
202–203: art by Raymond Perlman; photo by Jennie Lee Knight, National Audubon Society (°)

LIVING TOGETHER:

204–205: Bob Kuhn
206–207: Stanley Washburn (°)
208–209: Joseph Cellini
210–211: Edwin Way Teale
212–213: (*left*) Herbert Friedmann (°); (*right*) Eric Hosking, National Audubon Society (°)
214–215: art by Guy J. Coheleach; photo by Ross E. Hutchins (°)
216–217: art by Joseph Cellini; photo by L. J. Palmer, U.S. Department of Interior (°)
218–219: Chicago Natural History Museum (°)
220–221: Jerry Greenberg (°)
222–223: Devereux Butcher Photography (°)

QUEER, QUAINT, AND CURIOUS:

224–225: Stan Galli
226–227: Guy J. Coheleach
228–229: (*left*) Robert C. Hermes (°); (*right*) Ross E. Hutchins (°), Ralph Buchsbaum (°)
230–231: art by Raymond Perlman; photo by Ross E. Hutchins (°)
232–233: Bob Kuhn
234–235: (*left*) James N. Layne (°); (*right*) Robert C. Hermes (°)
236–237: (*left*) Roy Pinney (°); (*right*) Ylla, Rapho-Guillumette (°)

SAVING WHAT WE HAVE:

238–239: Charles Moser
240–241: Charles Edmonson
242–243: (*left, top to bottom*) Allan D. Cruickshank, NAS (°); Bill Gabriel, Photo Researchers (°); Alfred M. Bailey, NAS (°); (*right*) Wisconsin Conservation Department (°)
244–245: (*top*) New York State Department of Commerce (°); (*left*) Bermuda News Bureau (°); Devaney, Pix from Publix (°)
246–247: U.S. Forest Service (°)
248–249: (*left*) Minnesota Department of Business Development (°); (*right*) Devaney, Pix from Publix (°)
250–251: (*left*) Union Pacific Railroad (°): (*right*): (*top*) Canadian Pacific (°); (*center, left to right*) Darwin Vancampen, DPI (°); Jack Zehrt, Shostal (°); (*bottom, left to right*) Shostal (°); Murry Weiss, DPI (°)

LIVING ON A FARM:

252–253: H. A. Aldridge and George Lopac—Stephens Biondi De Cicco Inc.
254–255: art by Robert Addison—Stevens-Gross Studios, Inc.; photo by Grant Heilman (°)
256–257: Grant Heilman (°)
258–259: photo, The Wool Bureau (°); art by Bob Kuhn

260–261: Grant Heilman (°)
262–263: art by Keith Ward; photo by Grant Heilman (°)
264–265: Grant Heilman (°)
266–267: René Martin
268–269: Grant Heilman (°)
270–271: (*left*) CHILDCRAFT photo by James R. Simon; (*right*) Australian News and Information Bureau

OUT OF THE GROUND:

272–273: Mary Horton
274–275: art by Carl Yates; photo by John H. Gerard, NAS (°)
276–277: art by Carl Yates; photos (*left to right*) Illinois Natural History (°), U.S. Forest Products Laboratory Forest Service, U.S. Department of Agriculture (°)
278–279: James Teason
280–281: Carl Yates
282–283: photo by Lynwood Chase, NAS (°); art by Donald Charles
284–285: photo by John H. Gerard, NAS (°); art by James Teason
286–287: (*left*) CHILDCRAFT photo by Russell Kay; (*right*) Grant Heilman (°)
288–289: Carl Yates
290–291: James Teason

THINGS THAT HAPPEN TO ME:

292–293: Mary Horton
294–295: John Alcorn
296–297: John Henry—Stephens Biondi De Cicco Inc.
298–299: Hank Ketcham
300–301: Chicago's Free Fair, Back of the Yards Neighborhood Council (°)
302–303: art by Paul McNear; photo by Rie Gaddis
304–305: Don Stebbing
306–307: Robert Addison—Stevens-Gross Studios, Inc.
308–309: Robert Borja
310–311: CHILDCRAFT photo by E. F. Hoppe; art by Hans W. Bobzein
312–313: Susan Perl

HOW ANIMALS ACT:

314–315: Bob Kuhn
316–317: Guy J. Coheleach
318–319: Carroll Seghers II (°)
320–321: Guy J. Coheleach
322–323: (*left*) Ewing Galloway (°); (*right*) Hugh Davis (°), Ed Park, Three Lions (°), Western Photo & Science Service (°)
324–325: Ernst Huber, Conzett & Huber (°)
326–327: (*left*) John Warham (°); (*right*) Bryden Taylor, National Audubon Society (°)
328–329: photo by Mike Davis, Miami Gardens Fisheries (°); art by Guy J. Coheleach
330–331: Paul McNear
332–333: Charles Harper
334–335: Ross E. Hutchins (°)
336–337: Cy La Tour (°)

ABOUT ME AND OTHERS:

338–339: Gyo Fujikawa
340–341: Paul and Everett McNear
342–343: (*top left*) James H. Brown, (*bottom left*) H. W. Nowell, Black Star (°); (*right*) Robert Addison—Stevens-Gross Studios, Inc.
344–345: (*left*) James H. Brown; (*right*) James H. Brown, James H. Brown, Ross E. Hutchins (°)
346–347: photo by James H. Brown; art by Cal Roy—Swan Studios, Inc.
348–349: photo, Rie Gaddis; art by Art Magee—Magee Studio, Inc.
350–351: sculpture by Arnold Ryan Chalfant & Associates and Richard Rush Studios; photos by James H. Brown
352–353: photo by James H. Brown; sculpture by Arnold Ryan Chalfant & Associates and Richard Rush Studios
354–355: photo by James H. Brown; art by Paul McNear
356–357: Art Magee—Magee Studio, Inc.
358–359: James H. Brown
360–361: Charles Harper

Index to Volume 4

This index lists plants and animals by their common names. After each common name, the name of the plant or animal group is included in parentheses. For example, when you look up the entry "cat," you will see Cat (mammal) and the page numbers on which you will find material about cats. The members of an animal family, such as the cat family, are listed below the entry as *See also* Bobcat; Jaguar; Leopard; Lion; Lynx; Puma; Tiger.

Plants and animals found in other volumes of CHILDCRAFT are listed in the general CHILDCRAFT index in Volume 15.